Mormo Masonry, and Godhood:

Can Angels Be Trusted?

Dr. Cathy Burns

Sharing
212 E. 7th St. (O2)
Mt. Carmel, PA 17851-2211

Copyright 1997, by Cathy Burns. Published by Sharing.
Second Printing: 2003

All rights reserved. This book is protected under the copyright laws of the United States of America. This book may not be copied or reprinted for commercial gain or profit. Short quotations or occasional page copying for personal or group study is permitted and encouraged.

All Scripture quotations are from the King James Version of the Holy Bible.

ISBN: 1-891117-01-7

TABLE OF CONTENTS

1. Mormonism and Its History... 5

2. Some Doctrines of Mormonism... 32

3. Joseph Smith and Magic.. 54

4. Mormonism and Godhood.. 66

5. Parallels Between Mormonism... 82

Endnotes... 102

Bibliography... 113

Index... 118

Chapter One

MORMONISM AND ITS HISTORY

The founder of Mormonism, Joseph Smith, was born on December 23, 1805 in Sharon, Vermont. When Joe (as he was called) was about 14, his family moved to Manchester, New York. Lucy Mack, Joe's mother, had visions and practiced magic. Her husband, Joseph, Sr., was an avid treasure-hunter who was always trying to locate Captain Kidd's booty. His son, Joe, would often accompany him on these treasure hunts. Joe himself was known for being lazy, lying, and exaggerating, as well as having an attraction to several occult practices, including fortune telling and divining. Although millions of Mormons have revered Joseph Smith, those who knew the Smith family were not so gracious. The neighbors viewed the Smiths as "illiterate, whiskey-drinking, shiftless, and irreligious."[1]

One day in 1820 when Joseph, Jr., was 14 years old we are told, that he was stirred by a revival that had broken out in the vicinity of Palmyra, NY. Not knowing what to do, he went out into the woods and knelt down to pray. This was the first time that he ever prayed out loud. Immediately a bright light shone about him and he reported that God and His Son, Jesus, appeared unto him. Joseph asked these heavenly beings what church was the right one and which one he should join. He was told that he should not join any church as all the churches were wrong and that their creeds were an abomination in God's sight.[2]

6   MORMONISM, MASONRY, AND GODHOOD

This vision is very important to Mormonism because it is from this vision that Mormonism was started. Bruce McConkie, a leading Mormon, tells us: "This vision was the MOST IMPORTANT EVENT that had taken place in all world history from the day of Christ's ministry to the glorious hour when it occurred."[3] Paul R. Cheesman states: "Thus the Church of Jesus Christ of Latter-day Saints and THE STORY OF JOSEPH SMITH MUST STAND OR FALL ON THE AUTHENTICITY OF THE FIRST VISION and the appearance of the Angel Moroni."[4] (Emphasis mine throughout)

Since Mormonism is dependent on this vision, we need to look at what Joseph Smith claimed in this vision. He said that he was stirred by a revival that took place in 1820. Investigation was done in this area and it was discovered that there were no revivals in the Palmyra vicinity in 1820. In fact, no revival occurred in that area until the fall of 1824, so Smith's statement of what happened in his vision IS NOT TRUE![5]

Robert McKay presents another problem with Joseph's "vision." He writes:

"As canonized by the Mormon church, the account tells us that Joseph Smith was born in 1805, and moved to Palmyra, New York, at the age of 10 (1815). About four years later (1819), the family moved again, this time to Manchester. Among those listed as members of the family at the time of the move to Manchester is Joseph's sister Lucy **(Pearl of Great Price,** JS-H 1:3-5).

"It is with Lucy that the problem begins. Remember that the chronology provided by Joseph puts the family, including Lucy, in Manchester in 1819. However, Lucy was not born until July 18, 1821 **(Biographical Sketches of Joseph Smith the Prophet, and His Progenitors for Many Generations,** pg. 41).

This is over a year **after** the First Vision supposedly occurred in 1820. Thus, we have Joseph Smith presenting his sister Lucy as having been born **before** the First Vision, but giving a chronology which requires her to have been born the year **after** the vision."[6] (Emphasis in the original)

After this so-called First Vision Joseph tells us that:

"...having been forbidden to join any of the religious sects of the day, and being of very tender years...I was left to all kinds of temptations; and, mingling with all kinds of society, I frequently fell into many foolish errors, and displayed the weakness of youth, and the foibles of human nature; which, I am sorry to say, led me into divers temptations, offensive in the sight of God....In consequence of these things, I often felt condemned for my weakness and imperfections...."[7]

While Joseph seems to be "repentant" of his former lifestyle, it should be pointed out that in 1825 when he was 19, he "in less than a year will find himself in court charged with vagrancy and fraud and before a second year has expired eloping with a young woman from Pennsylvania."[8] In spite of his sinful living during this period, Joseph was supposedly receiving further visions from another being.

GOLD PLATES AND SILVER BOWS

On the night of September 21, 1823, after retiring to bed, he began to pray for forgiveness of his sins and also asked for a manifestation that he might know his standing before God. He was certain that he again would receive a manifestation as he had several years before. Sure enough, a light appeared in his room and he saw an angel standing in the air. This angel's name was Moroni.[9] He was a resurrected being who had lived

8 MORMONISM, MASONRY, AND GODHOOD

as a mortal here on earth. Moroni was the last prophet of the Nephite nation (one of the supposedly ancient inhabitants of America) and he was the last person to have written in the *Book of Mormon*. He told Joseph that he had buried this record in the side of a hill called Cumorah near Joseph's home in Palmyra, New York. Joseph Smith described this visit as thus:

"He called me by name, and said unto me that he was a messenger sent from the presence of God to me, and that his name was Moroni; that God had a work for me to do....

"He said there was a book deposited, written upon gold plates, giving an account of the former inhabitants

MORMONISM AND ITS HISTORY   9

of this continent, and the source from whence they sprang. He also said that the fulness of the everlasting Gospel was contained in it, as delivered by the Savior to the ancient inhabitants.

"Also, that there were two stones in silver bows—and these stones, fastened to a breastplate, constituted what is called the Urim and Thummim—deposited with the plates; and the possession and use of these stones were what constituted 'seers' in ancient or former times; and that God had prepared them for the purpose of translating the book."[10]

After relating these "truths" to Joseph Smith, Moroni was taken back up into heaven. As Joseph lay on the bed, reflecting on this visit, Moroni appeared again. He said the same things as he had said on the first visit and added that great judgments were coming upon the earth, and again ascended.

To Joseph Smith's surprise, Moroni appeared the third time and again repeated what he had said before and added that Satan would try to tempt him to get the plates for monetary reasons but that Joseph's objective should be only to get the plates for the glory of God. Then, for the third time that night, Moroni disappeared. The next day Moroni again appeared to Joseph and shortly afterwards, Joseph went to the place where the messenger had told him that the gold plates were deposited.[11]

MAGIC STONES

Under a large stone was a box which contained the gold plates, the Urim and Thummim, and the breastplate. As Joseph tried to withdraw these items, Moroni appeared to him and forbade him to do so. The messenger told him that he could not remove the plates for four more years but that he should come back to this place in precisely one year and once again meet with the messenger. Joseph was to continue to return at yearly intervals until he was allowed to have the plates. On September 22, 1827, Moroni delivered these plates, along with the breastplate, to him and Joseph began translating these plates with the aid of two magic stones called the Urim and Thummim. Bible scholars do not really know what the Urim and the Thummim really are, but Joseph Smith, an illiterate boy, claims that they were MAGIC stones and that he used them.

After Joseph Smith had copied off some of the characters and translated them, Martin Harris took the characters and the translation of them to Professor Anthon in New York. Mr. Harris claims that Professor Anthon stated that the translation was correct and that the characters were from the Egyptian, Chaldaic, Assyriac, and Arabic languages. Professor Anthon then supposedly presented Mr. Harris with a certificate to prove the authenticity of the translation. However, as Mr. Harris was leaving Professor Anthon's place, he called Mr. Harris back and asked him how Joseph Smith found these golden plates. Mr. Harris said that an angel of God had revealed it unto him. Professor Anthon then asked to see the certificate that he had given to Mr. Harris and proceeded to tear it up, saying that there was no such thing as the ministering of angels. (This is Mr. Harris' version of the story. However, when Professor Anthon received word of Smith's claim, he wrote a letter to Mr. Howe to tell his side of the story. In the letter he stated: "The whole story about my having pronounced the Mormonite inscription to be 'reformed Egyptian hieroglyphics' is perfectly false." He went on to tell how Mr. Harris had come to him and how he had tried to persuade Mr. Harris that these "golden plates" were a hoax or a trick. The characters that Mr. Harris showed him were anything but Egyptian, he said. He ended his letter to Mr. Howe with these words: "I have thus given you a full statement of all that I know respecting the origin of Mormonism, and must beg you, as a personal favor, to publish this letter immediately should you find my name mentioned again by these wretched fanatics."[12] It is easy to see that Professor Anthon's and Mr. Harris' stories do not coincide.)

GOLDEN SPECTACLES

Shortly after Mr. Harris' visit to Professor Anthon, Joseph Smith started the translation of the *Book of Mormon* with Oliver Cowdery. This translation was done by means of a large pair of "gold spectacles" that came with the plates. These spectacles were so enormous that a person could only look

through one of the lenses at a time. On May 15, 1829, a few weeks after the translation started, Smith and Cowdery went into the woods to pray and inquire of the Lord about the doctrine of baptism for the remission of sins that they found mentioned in the translation. As they prayed a messenger from heaven descended in a cloud of light and, laying his hands upon them, ordained them into the Aaronic Priesthood. He also commanded that they should baptize each other. This messenger identified himself as John the Baptist and told them that he acted under the direction of Peter, James, and John. These latter three held the keys of the Priesthood of Melchizedek, which office would also be bestowed upon Joseph Smith and Oliver Cowdery in the future.

MORMON CHURCH CONFLICTS WITH SCRIPTURE

As commanded by John the Baptist, Joseph Smith and Oliver Cowdery baptized each other and the Holy Ghost fell upon them and they began to prophesy. With their minds now being enlightened, they were able to understand the true meaning and intention of the scriptures.[13] They were also commanded to organize a church, so on April 6, 1830, the "Church of Jesus Christ of Latter-day Saints" (or Mormons) came into being. This church now has almost 10 million members and is the fifth largest church in the United States and Canada.

The Mormon Church claims to be of the Christian faith. One of the leading Mormons claims: "Mormonism is Christianity. Christianity is Mormonism. They are one and the same...."[14]

> "Mormons seem to forget that Joseph Smith declared all Christian creeds to be an abomination. Brigham Young said that all Christians were 'grovelling in darkness,' and that the Christian God is 'the Mormon's Devil....' John Taylor, third Mormon President, said that Christianity was 'hatched in hell,' and 'a perfect pack of nonsense...the Devil could not invent a better engine to spread his work....' Continuously around the world,

hundreds of times each day in secret ceremonies before thousands of Mormon Temple patrons, all Christian ministers are ridiculed and slandered as absolute fools who are hired by Satan to deceive their congregations....

"If Christianity were indeed 'hatched in hell' and the Christian God is 'the Mormon's Devil,' then the change in tactics that now has Mormon missionaries protesting to Christians, 'Our God is the same as your God,' is extremely dishonest....If Christianity were not 'hatched in hell,' then Mormonism was."[15]

However, the Mormons do not adhere strictly to the Bible. LeGrand Richards, a Mormon apostle, writes:

"The position of The Church of Jesus Christ of Latter-day Saints, or Mormon Church, will be discussed from the point of view that it is the only Christian church that **DOES NOT DEPEND ENTIRELY UPON THE BIBLE** for its teachings."[16]

Another Mormon brochure tells us that the Latter-day Saints have three other books—the *Book of Mormon,* the *Doctrine and Covenants,* and the *Pearl of Great Price.* "The teachings found in them," says the Mormon pamphlet, "do not conflict with the teachings of the Bible."[17] "Bible doctrine is

Mormon doctrine, and Mormon doctrine is Bible. They are one and the same."[18] Since Mormons claim their supplemental "scriptures" do not conflict with the Bible, let's take a look at one of these additions—the *Book of Mormon*.

DEAD SONS COME TO AMERICA?

Mormon literature states: "The *Book of Mormon* is the word of God. It is scripture."[19] It was supposedly written by prophets of God who lived in Palestine and America. This book contains the story of three migrations to the Americas. The first migration is recorded as happening about 2,250 B.C. A group called the Jaredites left the Tower of Babel at the time of the confusing of the languages. They were supposedly led to America by the Lord but they were not a peaceable people. They fought each other until only two people, Coriantumr and Shiz, remained. Then Coriantumr cut off Shiz's head.

The second group that migrated to the West were Lehi and his family. At the Lord's command the prophet Lehi and his son Nephi crossed the ocean to America around 600 B.C. Because of the wickedness of Lehi's sons, Laman and Lemuel, the Lord cursed them by making their skin black. These black-skinned people were called Lamanites in the *Book of Mormon* and supposedly became known as the American Indians. According to the Mormons, the American Indians "are of the house of Israel"[20] or Israelites, which is contrary to the Bible and to archaeological evidence. Soon these people were joined by the third migratory group. When King Zedekiah's dynasty collapsed, one of his sons, Mulek, and his followers also came to America. (Of course, the Bible tells us that King Zedekiah's sons were killed when his kingdom fell [see II Kings 25:7], so Zedekiah's sons could not have made it to America, but it doesn't matter to the Mormons that the boys were dead.) The families of Lehi and Mulek eventually merged into one nation.

MORMONISM AND ITS HISTORY 15

In 34 A.D., after His crucifixion and ascension, Jesus supposedly appeared unto these people and taught them about

baptism, the priesthood, and communion. The *Book of Mormon* then relates that in 385 A.D. a battle took place near the hill of Cumorah and everyone was killed except Moroni, the son of Mormon. After Moroni died it is claimed that he became an angel and appeared to Joseph Smith on the night of September 21, 1823, telling Joseph where he had hid the *Book of Mormon.* He told Joseph that this book contained "the fulness of the everlasting Gospel."

"WHY SHOULD THE WORLD DOUBT?"

To help prove that Joseph Smith did see the angel and the plates, three other men (Martin Harris, Oliver Cowdery, and David Whitmer) were also allowed to see them. Their testimony, known as the "Testimony of Three Witnesses" appears in the preliminary pages of every *Book of Mormon*. This testimony states in part: "And we declare with words of soberness, that an angel of God came down from heaven, and he brought and laid before our eyes, that we beheld and saw the plates, and the engravings thereon...."[21] Mormons also claim that eight other men were allowed to see and handle the plates and that their testimony is also contained in the front of the *Book of Mormon*.[22] LeGrand Richards, a Mormon apostle, states in his book, *A Marvelous Work and a Wonder:* "Each of these three witnesses passed from this life to meet his reward with a confirmation of the truth of his testimony upon his lips. Why should the world doubt?"[23]

That's a good question: "Why should the world doubt?" We should doubt this testimony for several reasons. One reason is that the Mormons fail to add that Mr. Harris later admitted that he had never seen the plates because they "were covered over with a cloth" and that Mr. Cowdery and Mr. Whitmer were later accused of THEFT AND COUNTERFEITING and had to leave the Mormon church and that Joseph Smith later denounced all three of them.[24] In *The Doctrine and Covenants* we find that Smith "states that Cowdery cannot be trusted unless 'one go with him who will be true and faithful' (69:1), and Martin Harris is called a 'wicked man' (3:12)."[25]

Mr. Richards claims that each of these men died with the testimony upon his lips, but this is not the case at all. The Bible tells us: "A faithful witness will not lie: but a false witness will utter lies" (Proverbs 14:5). Since Martin Harris lied he is a false witness. What about the eight other witnesses? Well, five of them were related to David Whitmer (the counterfeiter) and the other three were Joseph Smith's father and two brothers.

These are hardly objective witnesses especially knowing the Smith family's background of drunkenness and MAGIC!

A second reason to doubt is that Galatians 1:8 warns us that even if an angel from heaven would preach another doctrine than written in the Bible, he should be accursed. Moroni obviously preached a different and contrary doctrine, so we should not accept Mormonism's testimony. Another reason why the world has a good reason to doubt is that Deuteronomy 4:2; Proverbs 30:6; and Revelation 22:18-19 warn us that we are not to add to God's Word and the *Book of Mormon* is such an addition. Of course, one of the Mormon "Articles of Faith" states: "We believe the Bible to be the Word of God as far **as it is translated correctly....**"[26] Keeping in step with this view Mormon LeGrand Richards defends these additional writings by stating:

> "At first reading [of Revelation 22:18-19], one might be justified in assuming that the apostle John meant that no other scripture would be added to the Bible, and this particularly in view of the fact that it is contained in the last chapter of the Bible as we now have it. It is easy to understand, however, that this interpretation **IS ERRONEOUS....**"[27]

THE CHANGING BOOK

Although the *Book of Mormon* claims to be an **ADDITIONAL REVELATION** to the Bible, it contains over 300 verses from the King James Bible **WORD FOR WORD** even though it was supposed to have been written many centuries earlier. For example, I compared several chapters of the *Book of Mormon* to the Bible. I found that II Nephi 12:1-22 contained 8 verses that were **IDENTICAL** to Isaiah 2:1-22; II Nephi 13:1-26 had 12 verses **WORD FOR WORD** with

18 MORMONISM, MASONRY, AND GODHOOD

Isaiah 3:1-26; and II Nephi 24:1-32 had 18 verses **WORD FOR WORD** with Isaiah 14:1-32. The other verses in these chapters were **ALMOST IDENTICAL,** sometimes containing only **ONE LETTER** or **ONE WORD** that was different. Other passages throughout this book took portions of verses word for word from the Bible.

Even the archaeological finds are not in agreement with what is claimed in the *Book of Mormon.* One group of 10 researchers (9 of whom are Mormons) did investigation into the *Book of Mormon* and came to the conclusion that "the weight of linguistic, textual, archaeological and other evidence places the origin of the Book of Mormon squarely in the 19th century."[28] Smith's claim that this book was based on writings from the gold plates in 600 B.C. just doesn't fit. These researchers added "that existing geographical and archaeological evidence in Mesoamerica does not 'achieve even a partial fit' with Book of Mormon civilizations."[29]

Additionally:

"No Mormon cities in the Book of Mormon have been found. No Hebrew inscriptions have been found in Indian ruins. No ancient copies of transcripts or manuscripts (or pieces) of the Book of Mormon have

MORMONISM AND ITS HISTORY 19

ever been found. Historical facts contradict the Book of Mormon."[30]

The Bible, on the other hand, has been proven again and again to be correct by archaeological discoveries.

In addition, although Moroni told Joseph Smith that the *Book of Mormon* contained "the fulness of the everlasting Gospel," this is far from correct. Robert McKay, a former Mormon, tells us that the *Book of Mormon:*

> "contradicts every major LDS [Latter-day Saints] doctrine—baptism for the dead, eternal progression, plural marriage, a total apostasy of the church, and plurality of gods. In spite of Joseph Smith's claim that it is correct, it has undergone over 4000 changes [not counting punctuation and capitalization] since 1830....Many of these changes have actually changed the doctrines taught by the *Book of Mormon*....
>
> "In fact, there is almost nothing in Mormonism today that was originally taught."

Joseph Smith said: "...I told the brethren that the Book of Mormon was the most correct of any book on earth, and the keystone of our religion and a man would get nearer to God by abiding by its precepts, than by any other book." Isn't it strange that this "perfect" book has had over 4000 changes? Which edition of *The Book of Mormon* will bring a person closer to God? How can a person be a true Mormon and follow the teachings of the Mormon church when "there is almost nothing in Mormonism today that was originally taught"?

ANGEL CRAZE

Seeing that an angel supposedly appeared to Joseph Smith perhaps it would be good to take a look at angels. *Time* magazine published a 1993 survey which stated that 69% of Americans believe that angels exist. 55% believe that God created higher beings with special powers to act as His agents on earth. 46% believe that each person has his or her own guardian angel. 49% believe that fallen angels exist and 32% claim that they have personally felt an angelic presence.

It is quite obvious that angels are the craze right now. Book after book mentions angelic encounters. One bookstore had over 50 different titles on the topic of angels. Catalogs are loaded with all kinds of angel paraphernalia. Stores carry different types of angel knickknacks. Magazines openly discuss angelic experiences. There is even a talking board (really an ouija board) designed to communicate with angelic beings. The whole world seems to be inundated with angels. *Time* magazine mentioned that even Hillary Clinton wears a gold angel pin when she needs help.

What is going on? What caused this astonishing and extraordinary interest in angels? Do angels really exist? Furthermore, who are these angelic beings and what is their purpose? Can all angels be trusted? What does the Bible say about angelic encounters?

DO ANGELS REALLY EXIST?

We know from the Bible that angels do exist. There are about 300 references to angels in the Old and New Testaments. From Genesis to Revelation passages can be found about angels. Colossians 1:16 reminds us that all principalities and powers (including angels) were created by and for Jesus Christ. Angels were intimately connected with many incidents in Christ's life. Hebrews 1:6 states: "Let all the angels of God worship Him" and the angels are His "ministering spirits" (Hebrews 1:14). The angels certainly assisted and protected Christ many times throughout His life.

For instance, an angel appeared unto Mary to tell her that she was highly favored with the Lord and that she would give birth to Jesus (Luke 1:28-31). A short time later Joseph, to whom Mary was engaged, discovered that she was with child. He was going to put her away privately, but

> "while he thought on these things, behold, the angel of the Lord appeared unto him in a dream, saying, Joseph, thou son of David, fear not to take unto thee Mary thy wife: for that which is conceived in her is of the Holy Ghost" (Matthew 1:20).

At Christ's birth angels appeared to the shepherds to announce this magnificent occasion (Luke 2:9-15). When He was eight days old, He was given the name Jesus "which was so named of the angel before He was conceived in the womb" (Luke 2:21) because "He shall save His people from their sins" (Matthew 1:21).

Of course, when Herod, the king, found out that Jesus was born he wanted to kill Jesus. Again, an angel intervened and appeared to Joseph in a dream, saying: "Arise, and take the young child and His mother, and flee into Egypt, and be thou there until I bring thee word: for Herod will seek the young child to destroy Him" (Matthew 2:13). After Herod's death, the angel again came to Joseph with directions to return to Israel (Matthew 2:19-21).

When Satan tempted Christ in the wilderness, he said:

"If thou be the Son of God, cast thyself down: for it is written, He shall give His angels charge concerning thee: and in their hands they shall bear thee up, lest at any time thou dash thy foot against a stone" (Matthew 4:6; See also Luke 4:10).

After the temptations, angels came and ministered unto Christ (Matthew 4:11; Mark 1:13).

In the garden of Gethsemane we again see how the angels interacted with Christ. Jesus prayed saying: "Father, if thou be willing, remove this cup from Me: nevertheless not My will, but thine, be done" (Luke 22:42; See also Matthew 26:39). As He prayed "there appeared an angel unto Him from heaven, strengthening Him" (Luke 22:43).

Even at Christ's resurrection the angels were there. At the tomb, "the angel of the Lord descended from heaven, and came and rolled back the stone from the door, and sat upon it" (Matthew 28:2). He then announced to the women: "Fear not ye: for I know that ye seek Jesus, which was crucified. He is not here: for He is risen, as He said" (Matthew 28:5-6; See also Luke 24:23 and John 20:12).

The angels will also appear with Jesus when He comes again. "For the Son of man shall come in the glory of His Father with His angels; and then He shall reward every man

MORMONISM AND ITS HISTORY 23

according to his works" (Matthew 16:27; See also Matthew 25:31; 13:41, 49; 24:31; Mark 8:38; 13:27; and II Thessalonians 1:7).

ARE ALL ANGELS GOOD?

We've just seen from the Scriptures that angels do exist and that they are sent forth as ministering spirits, so now we need to know if all angels are good and if all of them can be trusted. The Bible, once again, gives us our answer and reveals that there are both good and evil angels. When Lucifer, the anointed cherub, decided that he would be like God, a third of the angels followed him (see Revelation 12:4 in conjunction with Isaiah 14:12-15 and Ezekiel 28:12-19). Revelation 12:7-9 explains:

> "And there was war in heaven: Michael and his angels fought against the dragon; and the dragon fought and his angels, And prevailed not; neither was their place found any more in heaven. And the great dragon was cast out, that old serpent, called the Devil, and Satan, which deceiveth the whole world: he was cast out into the earth, and his angels were cast out with him."

Christ said in Luke 10:18 that He "beheld Satan as lightning fall from heaven." Because of Satan's fall, hell was prepared for the devil and his angels (Matthew 25:41). II Peter 2:4 also reminds us that "God spared not the angels that sinned, but cast them down to hell, and delivered them into chains of darkness, to be reserved unto judgment" and Jude 1:6 states: "The angels which kept not their first estate, but left their own habitation, He hath reserved in everlasting chains under darkness unto the judgment of the great day." "And they had a king over them, which is the angel of the bottomless pit, whose name in the Hebrew tongue is Abaddon, but in the Greek tongue hath his name Apollyon" (Revelation 9:11).

The angels who followed Lucifer (who is Satan) are also called fallen angels, demons (or devils), and evil spirits. However, at present, not all evil angels are confined to hell. There are some angels who are promoting Satan's evil plans. These angels will bring false doctrines. I Timothy 4:1 tells us: "Now the Spirit speaketh expressly, that in the latter times some shall depart from the faith, giving heed to seducing spirits, and doctrines of devils." Of course, these evil angels don't appear as evil beings. If they did, most people would have nothing whatsoever to do with them. On the other hand, if angelic encounters seem pleasant and **appear** to be good, then people can easily be deceived by them. I Timothy 4:1 clearly states that some angels are **SEDUCING spirits.** These angels will fascinate, entice, and tantalize you in order to be able to ensnare and entangle you in their trap. In fact, II Corinthians 11:14 explains that "Satan himself is transformed into an angel of light" and that his ministers will do the same thing. This is why the Scriptures so clearly warn us to "believe not every spirit, but **try the spirits** whether they are of God: for many false prophets are gone out into the world" (I John 4:1).

MIRACLES OF GOD DUPLICATED

These evil spirits have great power and in some cases can even mimic the miracles of God. For example, the Word of God shows us that sinners (controlled by evil spirits) can and do perform miracles and that many people are deceived because of these miracles. In Exodus we find that God called Moses to go and speak to Pharaoh on behalf of the Israelites.

"And the Lord spake unto Moses and unto Aaron, saying, When Pharaoh shall speak unto you, saying, Shew a miracle for you: then thou shalt say unto Aaron, Take thy rod, and cast it before Pharaoh, and it shall become a serpent. And Moses and Aaron went in unto Pharaoh, and they did so as the Lord had commanded: and Aaron cast down his rod before Pharaoh, and before his servants, and it became a serpent. Then Pharaoh also called the wise men and the sorcerers: **NOW THE MAGICIANS OF EGYPT, THEY ALSO DID IN LIKE MANNER WITH THEIR ENCHANTMENTS.** For they cast down every man his rod, and they became serpents: but Aaron's rod swallowed up their rods" (Exodus 7:8-12).

The next chapter gives us another miracle that these magicians **DUPLICATED:** "And Aaron stretched out his hand over the waters of Egypt; and the frogs came up, and covered the land of Egypt. And the magicians did so with their enchantments, and brought up frogs upon the land of Egypt" (Exodus 8:6-7). So the magicians in Egypt reproduced at least two of the miracles that Moses and Aaron did. Because Pharaoh's magicians could do the same miracles as Moses and Aaron, his heart was hardened. There came a time, however, that Pharaoh's men could not duplicate the miracles, but this is one proof that evil spirits can and do perform miracles, even to the extent of performing the **EXACT SAME** miracles that a child of God can perform.

TRY THE SPIRITS

As was just mentioned, the Bible says that we are to try the spirits but this does not mean that just because a miracle or supernatural sign occurs, that the spirit is of God. Deuteronomy 13:1-3 explains:

> "If there arise among you a prophet, or a dreamer of dreams, and **GIVETH THEE A SIGN OR A WONDER, AND THE SIGN OR THE WONDER COME TO PASS,** whereof he spake unto thee, saying, Let us go after other gods, which thou hast not known, and let us serve them; Thou shalt not hearken unto the words of that prophet, or that dreamer of dreams: for the Lord your God proveth you, to know whether ye love the Lord your God with all your heart and with all your soul."

Here the Scripture plainly tells us that it is possible for a false prophet to give a sign and have it come to pass, but we are also told that we are not to believe the sign or wonder if it is to draw us away from serving the true God. The message given by Joseph Smith's angel was to draw people away from true Christianity, therefore neither the angel nor Joseph Smith should be followed regardless of any signs or wonders that may have come to pass.

Another instance of seducing spirits performing miracles is found in Matthew 24:24: "For there shall arise false Christs, and false prophets, and shall shew great **SIGNS AND WONDERS;** insomuch that, if it were possible, they shall deceive the very elect" (see also Mark 13:22). The miracles that these false prophets (under Satan's control) will perform will be so **OUTSTANDING** and **MARVELOUS** that even the elect must be on guard and take heed that they are not deceived by them. Paul, talking about the coming of the antichrist, explains that his "coming is after the working of Satan with all power and **SIGNS AND LYING WONDERS...**" (II Thessalonians 2:9). The book of Revelation also mentions several times that miracles will be performed by the false prophet in the last days. This false prophet will do "great wonders, so that he maketh fire come down from heaven on the earth in the sight of men, And deceiveth them that dwell on the earth by the means of those miracles which he had power to do in the sight of the beast..." (Revelation 13:13-14a). The three unclean spirits that come out of the mouths of the beast, the false prophet, and the dragon are described as "the spirits of devils, working miracles..." (Revelation 16:14).

THE MAJORITY IS NOT ALWAYS CORRECT

Also, just because the majority of people is following a prophet or an angel, does not mean that it is the right thing to do. In I Kings we find that King Ahab wanted to go to war against the Syrians so he called his 400 prophets together to see if he should go. All of these prophets said that he should go up and that the Syrians would be delivered into their hands and the battle would be prosperous. Finally one prophet of the Lord was called in and he said that Israel would be scattered as sheep without a shepherd. Ahab was quite angry over this but the prophet declared:

> "I saw the LORD sitting on his throne, and all the host of heaven standing by him on his right hand and on his left. And the LORD said, Who shall persuade Ahab, that he may go up and fall at Ramoth-gilead? And one said on this manner, and another said on that manner. And there came forth a spirit, and stood before the LORD, and said, I will persuade him. And the LORD said unto him, Wherewith? And he said, I will go forth, and **I will be a lying spirit in the mouth of all his prophets.** And he said, Thou shalt persuade him, and prevail also: go forth, and do so" (I Kings 22:19-22; See also II Chronicles 18:18-21).

Here were 401 prophets but only 1 of them was telling the truth. The majority is not always correct. We cannot just jump on a bandwagon because of popularity. We must **carefully** and **prayerfully** consider the course we plan to take and see if it lines up with the Word of God. If it doesn't, it doesn't matter how many people are pursuing it. We cannot compromise God's Word and be held guiltless.

There is an angel craze today but most all of the angels appearing are not of God. True angels of God will **NEVER** go against God's Word. Earlier I mentioned that magazines are loaded with angel paraphernalia. These magazines, however, are usually New Age or occult publications. The books dealing with angels are most often channeled material (which is a practice forbidden by Deuteronomy 18:10-12) or contain so-called angelic encounters that don't line up doctrinally with the Bible. The talking board used to contact angels is a form of divination which is also condemned numerous times in the Scriptures.

MORMONISM AND ITS HISTORY   29

TRUE ANGELIC PROTECTION

Angels are watching over God's children. Psalm 91:11 states: "He shall give His angels charge over thee, to keep thee in all thy ways." "The angel of the Lord encampeth round about them that fear Him, and delivereth them" (Psalm 34:7), but we are not to seek communication with angels. There are several examples of this type of protection given in the Scriptures. When Daniel was thrown into the lion's den, he was unharmed because as Daniel said: "My God hath sent His angel and hath shut the lions' mouth, that they have not hurt me" (Daniel 6:22).

One time Peter was thrown into jail and Herod was planning to kill him, but many people were praying for Peter. Once again, God sent an angel who led Peter out of the prison and delivered him from Herod's evil intentions (Acts 12:1-19). When the three Hebrew children were cast into the fiery furnace because they would not fall down and worship an idol, we see that God "sent His angel, and delivered His servants that trusted in Him" (Daniel 3:28). There are several other instances mentioned in the Bible where God sent an angel to protect and deliver His children, but not once are we told that we should try to contact an angel or try to communicate with them. However, if the need arises, the **Lord Himself** will send an angel for reinforcement, deliverance, and protection. If we seek the Lord, He knows our needs and will supply them according to His purposes.

Colossians 2:18-19a specifically warns: "Let no man beguile you of your reward in a voluntary humility and worshipping of angels, intruding into those things which he hath not seen, vainly puffed up by his fleshly mind, And not holding the Head [Christ]." Those who are seeking after angels are ignoring Christ and following after things that are in opposition to Him and His Word. In fact, angels are popular, in part, because they are supposedly non-judgmental. With angel guidance, a person can persist in sin without worrying about being condemned for his or her lifestyle. On the other hand, God does disapprove of a sinful life and this causes guilt. Therefore, many people would prefer contact with angels rather than with God because a person feels that he can get away with more. This, however, is not true, for whether we like it or not, "we shall all stand before the judgment seat of Christ" (Romans 14:10). We may feel like we are getting away with sin now but a payday is coming.

Also, the current craze in angels is only another sign that Jesus is coming soon. As mentioned earlier, I Timothy 4:1 tells us that "in the **latter times** some shall depart from the faith, giving heed to seducing spirits, and doctrines of devils."

MORMONISM AND ITS HISTORY   31

The angel fad is preparing the world to accept the seducing doctrines of devils and to accept the worship of the beast. We must be careful not to be taken in by this fad but to continually seek the Lord with our whole heart.

With this brief study of angels, we can see that both bad and good angels exist. We can also see that the angel Moroni that appeared to Joseph Smith was an evil angel for the doctrines this angel taught are not compatible with Scriptures. In the next chapter we are going to look at some of the Mormon doctrines such as baptism for the dead, polygamy, sealed marriages, and who Lucifer's brother is, and compare them to the Bible, for "Every word of God is pure..." (Proverbs 30:5) and "though we, or an angel from heaven, preach **ANY OTHER GOSPEL** unto you than that which we have preached unto you, let him be accursed" (Galatians 1:8).

Chapter Two

SOME DOCTRINES OF MORMONISM

We've already looked at the history of the Mormon Church so let's turn our attention to some doctrines of Mormonism. Some of the Mormon beliefs include: baptism for the dead; the Aaronic and Melchizedek priesthoods; speaking in tongues; private revelations from God (which include revelations that are contradictory to the Bible); insistence that the U.S. Constitution is divinely inspired; secret temple ceremonies and Masonic-like rituals; binding temple oaths; all humans were spirit children before being born; we are not saved by faith alone; polygamy; God and Jesus had many wives; no literal hell with eternal punishment; God was once a man and man will one day become a God; universal salvation; and the belief that Jesus and Lucifer are brothers. Mormons also believe in a three-tiered heaven where there are separate sections for heathens, non-Mormon Christians, and those with sealed marriages. Additionally, Mormons have strange beliefs about God, Jesus Christ, and the Holy Spirit.

Let's look at some of these tenets in more detail. We'll start with the Mormons' view of God. The *Book of Mormon* (one of the "scriptures" of Mormonism) stated **ORIGINALLY** that God was eternal, unchangeable, and a spirit being.[1] Mormon 9:19 states: "...And behold, I say, unto you he changeth not; if so he would cease to be God; and he ceaseth not to be God, and is a God of miracles." However, through later "revelations," Joseph Smith declared that God had been a man:

"**God himself was once as we are now, and is an exalted Man,** and sits enthroned in yonder heavens...if you were to see him to-day, you would see him like a man in form."[2] Instructions given by Joseph Smith on April 2, 1843, included the following: "The Father has a body of flesh and bones as tangible as man's..." (*Doctrine and Covenants* 130:22). Lorenzo Snow coined the phrase that most popularly expresses this doctrine: "As man is, God once was. **As God is, man may become.**"[3] Mormonism fulfills the verse in Romans 1:22-23: "Professing themselves to be wise, they became fools, And changed the glory of the uncorruptible God into an image made like to corruptible man...."

WAS GOD A MAN?

The leader who followed Joseph Smith was Brigham Young. He stated: "God was once a man in mortal flesh as we are."[4] This Mormon "God" is not omnipresent (his body prohibits this), omnipotent, nor omniscient. He became God by obeying the Mormon "gospel" and in his rise to godhood he kept his physical body. Mormon Orson Pratt states: "The Gods who dwell in the Heaven...were once in a fallen state...their terrestrial bodies after suffering death, were redeemed, and glorified, and made Gods...they were exalted also, from fallen men to Celestial Gods."[5]

My Bible does not agree with this doctrine for it states "I am the Lord, I CHANGE NOT..." (Malachi 3:6).

Another Mormon, Bruce McConkie, declared "God himself, the Father of us all, is a glorified, exalted, immortal, resurrected Man"![6] He goes on to say that: "...the present exalted position of our Heavenly Father was gradually built up...if He should ever do anything to violate the confidence or 'sense of justice' of these intelligences, they would promptly withdraw their support, and the 'power' of God would disintegrate."⁷

This "God" had at least one and probably millions of wives. One day this "God" came from the planet Kolob into the Garden of Eden and eventually he became the first man, Adam. Brigham Young taught this doctrine openly from 1852 to his death in 1877. He said: "When our father Adam came into the Garden of Eden [in Missouri], he came into it with a CELESTIAL BODY, and brought Eve, **ONE OF HIS WIVES**, with him....He is Michael, THE ARCH-ANGEL, the Ancient of Days!...He is...the only God with whom we have to do."⁸

On June 14, 1873 he stated:

SOME DOCTRINES OF MORMONISM   35

"How much unbelief exists in the minds of Latter-day Saints [Mormons] in regard to one particular doctrine which I revealed to them, and which GOD REVEALED TO ME—namely that Adam is our father and god....Our father Adam helped to make this earth...he brought ONE OF HIS WIVES with him...who is he? He is Michael."[9]

This "God" cohabitated with his wife Eve and eventually fathered Jesus. Brigham Young tells us that this "God" is Father Adam. He said:

"When the Virgin Mary conceived the child Jesus, the Father had begotten him in his own likeness. He

was not begotten by the Holy Ghost. And who is the Father? He is the first of the human family; Jesus, our elder brother, was begotten in the flesh by the same character that was in the garden of Eden, and who is our Father in Heaven. Now, remember from this time forth, and for ever, that **Jesus Christ was not begotten by the Holy Ghost.**"[10]

Later in the *Journal of Discourses* we find: "The birth of the Savior was as natural as are the births of our children; it was the result of natural action."[11]

Former Mormon President, Orson Pratt, remarked: "Therefore, the Father and mother of Jesus according to the flesh, must have been associated together in the capacity of Husband and Wife; hence the Virgin Mary must have been for the time being, the lawful wife of God the Father."[12]

These statements are blasphemy for the Bible emphatically states: "She [Mary] was found with child of the Holy Ghost." The *Book of Mormon* (I Nephi 11:18) also states that Jesus was begotten "after the manner of the flesh" which means (according to the Mormons) that Jesus was not virgin-born.

OUR JESUS IS NOT THE MORMON'S "JESUS"

Jesus was not the only one who was fathered by God according to one Mormon brochure. This brochure explains:

> "...ALL men lived in a premortal estate before they were born into this world; ALL were born in the premortal existence as the spirit children of the Father. Christ was the firstborn spirit child; and from that day forward he has had preeminence in all things....Christ, the Word, the Firstborn, had, of course, attained unto the status of Godhood while yet in premortal existence."[13]

Although Mormons claim that their teachings "do not conflict with the teachings of the Bible,"[14] it is quite obvious that there is a conflict.

I think that it should be clear that the Jesus of Mormonism IS NOT the same Jesus that the Christians worship. One Mormon, Bernard Brockbank, even stated that "many of the Christian churches worship a DIFFERENT JESUS CHRIST than is worshipped by the Mormons."[15] A Mormon brochure entitled, *Christ in America,* by Elder Mark E. Petersen, gives us other names by which this "Christ" was known. Some of these names include: Quetzalcoatl (meaning "Plumed Serpent," or "Feathered Serpent"), Votan, Lono, Wixepechocha, Gucumatz, Sume, Kane, Kana, Kon, Kanaloa, Tongo-roa, Hyustus, Illa-Tici, and Viracocha. This "Viracocha," we are told in *World Religions: From Ancient History to the Present,* had three sons, one of whom was sent away and "became the underworld power of destruction....He was also the god of death and fertility...."[16] Does this sound like the Christ of the New Testament? Certainly not!

SALVATION BY WORKS INSTEAD OF FAITH

This Mormon Jesus was the spirit brother of Lucifer. According to Mormonism, both Jesus and Lucifer wanted to be the savior and when Lucifer's plan was rejected, Lucifer rebelled and took one-third of the heavenly host with him. In *The Gospel Through the Ages* we find: "The appointment of Jesus to be the Savior of the world was contested by one of the other sons of God. He was called Lucifer...this SPIRIT-BROTHER OF JESUS, desperately tried to become the Savior of mankind."[17] Mormon Bruce McConkie asserted: **"...Lucifer, the son of the morning, is our elder brother and brother of Jesus Christ."**[18]

Yet, at the Brigham Young University (BYU), McConkie stated that "part of Lucifer's system" was having a personal relationship with Jesus.[19] The *Doctrine and Covenants,* one of the Mormon "scriptures," states that "the idea that the Father and Son dwell in a man's heart is an old sectarian notion, and is false" (*Doctrine and Covenants* 130:3). Although Mormons claim that Jesus' plan was accepted, they certainly don't believe that we need His atonement. We are saved by faith alone but Mormon "scriptures" declare: "...we know that it is by grace that we are saved AFTER ALL THAT WE CAN DO."[20]

Mormon apostle, LeGrand Richards, writes:

"One **erroneous teaching** of many Christian churches is: *By faith alone we are saved.* This **false doctrine** would relieve man from the responsibility of his acts other than to confess a belief in God, and would teach man that no matter how great the sin, a confession would bring him complete forgiveness and salvation."[21]

Mormons, then, believe in SALVATION BY WORKS instead of salvation BY FAITH. This is unscriptural, but then, Brigham Young, the person who followed Joseph Smith in leadership of the Mormon church, confessed:

"...that he had 'not read the Bible for years' and that when he had attempted to study it, he 'did not understand the spirit and meaning of it....' He further admitted that in his day the Twelve Apostles of the Mormon Church included men who believed in reincarnation, rejected the existence of God, and denied that there was any value in the death of Christ for salvation. One would think that such admissions as these and the many others equally damaging that we have quoted would cause every Mormon to seriously reevaluate his religion."[22]

They also imply in their booklet, *What the Mormons Think of Christ,* that salvation through Christ's blood "is such utter nonsense and so palpably false that to believe it is to lose one's salvation."[23] The Bible tells us, however, that Christ's blood is precious: "Forasmuch as ye know that ye were not redeemed with corruptible things, as silver and gold...But with the PRECIOUS BLOOD of Christ..." (I Peter 1:18-19). With

SOME DOCTRINES OF MORMONISM 39

the supposed inadequacy of Christ's blood comes a strange Mormon doctrine known as "Blood Atonement." Mormons claim that **Christ's blood cannot atone for certain sins.** The only thing adequate to atone for these sins, such as murder, etc., would be the person's **OWN** blood. Another person could kill him as a righteous act that Brigham Young described as "loving our neighbor as ourselves...if he wants salvation and it is necessary to spill his blood...spill it."[24] The *Journal of Discourses* maintains: "There is not a man or woman, who violates covenants made with their God, that will not be required to pay their debt. The blood of Christ will never wipe that out. Your own blood must atone for it...."[25] This belief tries to do away with our sufficiency in Christ and His atonement.

MORMON JESUS IS A POLYGAMIST

This Jesus of Mormonism also was married. Orson Pratt says that "the great Messiah who was the founder of the Christian religion, was a Polygamist."[26] In fact, Brigham Young went so far as to say that the wedding at Cana was Jesus' own wedding where He married Mary and Martha. They also claim that He was married to Mary Magdalene.[27] Mormon Jedeliah Grant insists that Jesus' crucifixion came about because of His polygamy: "The grand reason of the burst of public sentiment in anathemas upon Christ and his disciples, causing his crucifixion, was evidently based on polygamy....A belief in the doctrine of a plurality of wives caused the persecution of Jesus and his followers."[28]

The Bible clearly tells us that Christ was crucified because He claimed to be the Son of God: "The Jews answered him [Pilate], We have a law, and by our law He ought to die, because He made Himself the Son of God" (John 19:7; see also Matthew 26:64-66; Mark 14:60-64; and Luke 22:66-71). We also know that the Bible states that adulterers cannot enter heaven, but Mormons claim that they can.

Originally, polygamy was considered to be a sin. The *Book of Mormon* said: "For there shall not any man among you have save it be one wife: and concubines he shall have none" (Jacob 2:27) and the 1835 edition of *Doctrine and Covenants* stated that fornication and polygamy were crimes.

SOME DOCTRINES OF MORMONISM   41

However, in 1843, Smith received a special "revelation" which allowed polygamy and this prohibition was deleted from 1876 on and in its place this book declared that polygamy was an "everlasting covenant."[29] Smith, of course, needed a "revelation" that would condone his wicked and adulterous behavior.

> "In 1841 Joseph Smith sent Henry B. Jacobs on a mission. While he was absent, Joseph seduced and married Jacobs' wife, Zina D. Huntington Jacobs. She became Joseph's 7th wife. One report states that when Jacobs returned from his mission he found his wife pregnant with Joseph's child. In 1846, after Joseph's death, Zina left Jacobs to marry Brigham Young, Mormonism's second Prophet. Brigham reportedly told Jacobs that since Zina had been Joseph's spiritual wife, and since Brigham was now Joseph's proxy, Zina and her children belonged to him (Brigham). He consoled Jacobs by telling him that he (Jacobs) could go and get a different wife for himself.
>
> "Of the 49 'wives' of Joseph Smith, 13 of them were married to other men at the time they married Joseph. He also married five pairs of sisters and one mother/daughter set (for a biblical perspective on this, see Lev. 18:17, 18; 20:14). Six of Joseph's wives had at one time been wards in his home and cared for by his legal wife, Emma."[30]

As just mentioned, Smith had 49 wives and his successor, Brigham Young, married 27 wives and had 56 children.[31]

This idea of polygamy even extended to the point of swapping wives.

> "Mormon John D. Lee wrote, 'Some have mutually agreed to exchange wives and have been sealed to

each other as husband and wife by virtue and authority of the holy priesthood. One of Brigham's brothers...made an exchange of wives with Mr. Decker....They both seemed happy in the exchange of wives.'"[32]

PROPHETS PROCLAIM POLYGAMY IS NECESSARY

Polygamy is a vital doctrine in Mormonism. Apostle George Teasdale said: "I bear my solemn testimony that plural marriage is as true as any principle that has been revealed from the heavens [through Joseph Smith—D.H. & E.D.]...."[33] Polygamy is such an important tenet of Mormonism that Orson Pratt, another Mormon Apostle, remarked: "If the doctrine of polygamy, as revealed to the Latter-day Saints, is not true, I would not give a fig for all your other revelations that came through Joseph Smith the Prophet; I would renounce the whole of them...."[34]

In fact, the Mormon's belief in polygamy is so significant that one's salvation is supposed to be based on it. Orson Pratt declared:

"...I have heard now and then...a brother or sister say, 'I am a Latter-day Saint, but I do not believe in polygamy.' Oh, what an absurd expression! What an absurd idea!

"A person might as well say, 'I am a follower of the Lord Jesus Christ, but I do not believe in him.' One is as consistent as the other....

"I did hope there was more intelligence among the Latter-day Saints, and a greater understanding of principle than to suppose that anyone can be a member of this Church in good standing and yet reject polygamy.

SOME DOCTRINES OF MORMONISM 43

"The Lord has said, that **those who reject this principle [of polygamy] reject their salvation, they shall be damned,** said the Lord...."³⁵

Mormon John J. Stewart said: "...seven of our nine Church presidents have lived plural marriage, and...this principle still is and always will be a doctrine of the Church."³⁶

With the endorsement of polygamy from the "prophets" and with a "revelation" from "God" that polygamy was necessary for their salvation, polygamy was openly practiced by the Mormons. However, in 1890, when the practice of polygamy prevented Utah from becoming a state, Fourth President of the Mormon Church, Wilford Woodruff, conveniently had another "revelation" that the "everlasting covenant" of polygamy was wrong, thus allowing Utah admittance into the Union.³⁷ Had polygamy been the "everlasting covenant" no "revelation" should have changed this, for Psalm 119:89 states: "For ever, O Lord, thy word is settled in heaven."

Woodruff, however, in spite of his "revelation," continued practicing polygamy (in violation of his promise to stop this practice) and reminded the Mormons: "If we were to do away with polygamy...then we must do away with prophets and Apostles, with revelation and the gifts and graces of the Gospel, and finally give up our religion altogether...."[38]

Although many Mormons deny that polygamy is still being practiced today, there are about 25,000 people who are still engaging in polygamy in Utah alone. As we have already seen, polygamy is a **NECESSARY** part of the Mormon religion. Not only is the Mormon's salvation based on this doctrine, but it is only through polygamy that one may attain godhood and become a God. Brigham Young told his followers: "The **ONLY** men who become gods are those who enter into polygamy."[39] It's no wonder, then, that a former Mormon has stated that "polygamy is alive and growing in Utah and the West."[40] However, even a Mormon who engages in polygamy cannot attain godhood UNLESS he has gone through a TEMPLE MARRIAGE.

TEMPLE MARRIAGE

Former Mormon, Robert McKay, states:

> "Among the things required for exaltation to godhood is TEMPLE MARRIAGE. Mormons believe that in an LDS [Latter-day Saint] temple a husband and wife can be sealed to each other so that the marriage (including sexual relations) will continue throughout eternity."[41]

In contrast to this belief we find that the Bible states in Mark 12:25 (and Matthew 22:30): "For when they shall rise from the dead, they neither marry, nor or given in marriage, but are as the angels which are in heaven." In spite of this,

SOME DOCTRINES OF MORMONISM 45

Mormons believe that this couple will be able to produce children in heaven because their marriage is now "sealed" for "time and eternity."

The sealing of marriages can also be done in proxy for the dead. This feature is so important to Mormons that the LDS temple in Portland, Oregon (which cost $22 million) "contains 127 rooms, including 14 sealing rooms and four ordinance rooms."[42] Mormon LeGrand Richards states:

> "Without such sealing ordinance of marriage, one cannot obtain the highest degree of celestial glory (D&C 131:1-4), 'which glory shall be a fulness and a continuation of the seeds for ever and ever' (D&C 132:19)."[43]

What is interesting is that sealing has a very significant role in Satanism. "The Mormon sealing is very similar to what is done in witchcraft called handfasting, and it is also similar to marriage sealing in Satanism."[44]

One author writes:

> "Joseph Smith, whose family practiced witchcraft, had many types of seals around their house which were

> used in magic. According to a magic book of 1830 <u>Demonology and Witchcraft</u> by Walter Scott (pp. 165, 220-221) seer stones were to be anointed with oil, and sealed with holy characters. In 1837, Mormon leaders performed such a magical sealing for James Colin Brewster. (<u>Mormonism & the Magic World View</u>, p. 209-210) Joseph Smith had a cane with a serpent on

the top of it, and astrological seals below. Magick staff or canes are important in Satanism. The seal of Mars was carved on the Smith family athame which was used by the family to draw circles for magic incantations."[45]

LIFE-LONG UNDERGARMENT

Ed Decker, a former Mormon, explains about the preparation for this sealing ceremony. He writes:

> "Husbands and wives joyfully anticipating having their marriage 'sealed' in the Temple for eternity are immediately parted and will only come together briefly after having endured two hours of rituals separate from each other. Led first to men's and women's dressing rooms, they are instructed to strip stark naked....
>
> "After partially covering their nudity with a poncho-like piece of thin cotton completely open on both sides, to which the key to their locker is pinned, the 'Temple patrons,' as they are called, are led to the 'washing and anointing' room. There Temple workers first ceremoniously 'wash' the various parts of their nude bodies with water, reaching under the open 'shield,' as it is called, and then 'anoint' the initiates with oil in a similar manner. During this startling process, a singsong formula is recited by the Temple worker bestowing a special blessing upon each body part being 'washed' or 'anointed.' This is the preparation for being dressed in the 'Garment of the Holy Priesthood,' a sort of 'magic underwear' much like an old-fashioned set of long johns with Masonic markings sewn into it. The Temple Worker recites:
>
> "'...having authority, I place this garment upon you [for and in behalf of (patron, then worker, both speak the name of the deceased), who is dead—D.H. & E.D.] which you must wear throughout your life.

SOME DOCTRINES OF MORMONISM

"'It represents the garment given to Adam when he was found naked in the Garden of Eden, and is called the Garment of the Holy Priesthood.

"'Inasmuch as you do not defile it, but are true and faithful to your covenants, it will be a shield and a protection to you against the power of the destroyer until you have finished your work here on earth.

"'With the garment I give you a new name, which you should always remember, and which you must keep sacred, and never reveal except at a certain place that will be shown you hereafter.

"'The name is _____.'"[46]

LeGrand Richards writes:

"The Lord intended that the marriage covenant should be for time and for all eternity and the practice of marrying 'until death do you part' did not originate with the Lord or his servants, but is a man-made doctrine. Therefore, all men and women who had died without having been sealed to each other for time and for all eternity, by the power of the holy priesthood, have no claim upon each other after they are dead. They also have no claim upon their children, for the children have not been born under the covenant of eternal marriage. In order that the purposes of the Lord should not be defeated and that he should not come 'and smite the earth with a curse', it became necessary, when the gospel was restored [through Joseph Smith] in this dispensation, for the keys of the priesthood also to be restored, whereby living children can be **VICARIOUSLY** married for the **DEAD PARENTS** and be sealed to them as their children, even as they can be baptized for them."[47]

BAPTISM FOR THE DEAD

But the practice of marrying "until death do you part" did originate with the Lord for we find in Romans 7:2: "For the woman which hath an husband is bound by the law to her husband SO LONG AS HE LIVETH; but if the husband be dead, SHE IS LOOSED from the law of her husband." In spite of plain Scriptural precepts Mormons engage in ceremonies for the dead which are performed in the Mormon temple. The

SOME DOCTRINES OF MORMONISM 49

temple is a special place and is not to be confused with the Mormon chapels. For instance, there are about 1000 chapels in California but only 2 temples in that state. The temples are secret places and are not open to the general public. There are 51 operating Mormon temples (worldwide) with 15 more in the process of being constructed or planned.[48] One of these temples is in Belmont, Massachusetts.[49] In May 1997 a new temple was opened in St. Louis, Missouri and another is scheduled to be opened this fall in Vernal, Utah.[50]

In *The Mormon Story* we are told:

"The Temples of the Church of Jesus Christ of Latter-day Saints are built for particular sacred ordinances....

"The ceremonies performed in the Temples by all members of good standing in the Church pertain to the salvation of **all** peoples who have died without a knowledge of the full Gospel of Jesus Christ. These ceremonies are based upon the belief that the soul of every person born into this life from the very beginning of time will, after death, yet live as an individual in a tangible resurrected state and **go on toward perfection.**

"**It is for universal salvation of all mankind who accept that full Gospel of Jesus Christ that the ordinances and ceremonies are performed in the Temples** by the living members for themselves first and then as proxies for those that have passed from this life into the next....Their belief is that all mankind has the privilege of eternal progression from this 'grade' of life to another, with each individual retaining his or her identity, and with the family unit remaining intact."[51]

One feature of Mormon temple work is **BAPTISM FOR THE DEAD.** LeGrand Richards states that this doctrine was received "by revelation and not by reading the Bible."[52] I think this is very obvious! Mormons believe that only Mormons can be saved. Since most people have never had a chance to accept Mormonism while they were alive, they are presented with the Mormon gospel in the spirit world. Then Mormons who are living now must be baptized **VICARIOUSLY** for them so that they are then allowed to progress toward becoming a God. The Bible clearly states in Hebrews 9:27 that "it is appointed unto men once to die, but after this the judgment." There is no "second chance" for salvation. Nonetheless, Mormons continue to be baptized on behalf of the dead hoping that these spirits will be granted another chance in the afterlife. In fact, they like to do about 150 to 200 baptisms **an hour** for the dead.[53]

It is claimed that 98% of all temple work is done on behalf of the dead. This work for the dead includes baptism; sealing of marriages; ordination in which the Aaronic and Melchizedic Priesthoods are bestowed upon males; and confirmation by which a dead person receives the Holy Ghost. Mormons trace their family records to find ancestral names and then go to the temple to be baptized by immersion for each of these people. The Bible warns: "Neither give heed to fables and endless genealogies, which minister questions, rather than godly edifying which is in faith..." (I Timothy 1:4).

SOME DOCTRINES OF MORMONISM 51

Time magazine states:

> "The importance of baptizing one's progenitors has led the Mormons to amass the fullest genealogical record in the world, the microfilmed equivalent of 7 million books of 300 pages apiece."[54]

It costs over $10 million a year to maintain these facilities. Most of these funds are received through the tithing of Mormon members. The Bible, however, **PROHIBITS ANY ONE** from giving **ANY** of their tithes for the dead (see Deuteronomy 26:12-14). In spite of the Biblical prohibition, some Mormons go through the 2-3 hour ceremony on behalf of a nonrelative that they never even knew. One newspaper clipping stated that one woman was baptized OVER 30,000 times![55] This proxy baptism is supposed to help both the Mormon and his dead relatives and friends to receive eternal life. Even though one Mormon Article of Faith states that "all mankind will be saved," only baptized Mormons can attain godhood.

We have seen that the doctrines of Mormonism are not to be found in the Bible, God's Holy Word.

HOW TO DISCERN A FALSE PROPHET

Another issue that needs to be looked at is Mormonism's claim that Joseph Smith was a prophet. The Bible reveals to us how to tell if a person is a true prophet of God or not. In Deuteronomy 18:21-22 it states:

> "And if thou say in thine heart, How shall we know the word which the Lord hath not spoken? When a prophet speaketh in the name of the Lord, if the thing follow not, nor come to pass, that is the thing which the Lord hath not spoken, but the prophet hath spoken it presumptuously: thou shalt not be afraid of him."

Just **ONE** incorrect prophecy makes a person a false prophet!

Even one of the official Mormon papers said this: "When, therefore any man, no matter who, or how high his standing may be, utters, or publishes, any thing that afterwards proves to be untrue, he is a false prophet."[56]

How did Joseph Smith line up in this area? In *Doctrine and Covenants* in September 1832, he said "that the new Jerusalem and its temple were to be built in Missouri in that specific generation, 'for verily **this generation shall not pass away** until a house shall be built unto the Lord.'"[57] This one "prophecy" alone proves that Smith is a false prophet (by both the Bible and the official Mormon article). He also said that the Second Coming would take place in 1891.[58] Of course, he also claimed that there were men on the moon and he proceeded to describe them. He said they were dressed like Quakers, were about six feet in height and lived nearly a 1000 years.[59]

However, even if any of Smith's prophecies did come to pass, this is still no guarantee that he was a man of God. As mentioned in the last chapter, Deuteronomy 13:1-3 says:

> "If there arise among you a prophet, or a dreamer of dreams, and giveth thee a sign or a wonder, And the sign or the wonder come to pass, whereof he spake unto thee, saying, Let us go after other gods, which thou hast not known, and let us serve them; Thou shalt not hearken unto the words of that prophet, or that dreamer of dreams...."

In other words, if a prophet gives a prophecy that comes to pass, but if that person is advocating the worship of other gods or teaching untrue doctrines, then he is still a false prophet. Smith obviously was teaching false tenets and things contrary to the Scriptures, so even if any of his "prophecies" were fulfilled, he was not sent by God.

In the next chapter we will look at the Smith family's involvement in magic. Even though Mormons believe that "all mankind will be saved," the Bible tells us: "Not every one that saith unto me, Lord, Lord, shall enter into the kingdom of heaven; but he that doeth the will of my Father which is in heaven" (Matthew 7:21).

Chapter Three

JOSEPH SMITH AND MAGIC

As I mentioned in Chapter 1, Joseph Smith's mother had visions and practiced magic. In fact: "Joseph Smith, Sr. and his entire family cast magic circles and practiced the 'faculty of Abrac,' according to Joseph Smith, Jr.'s *own mother,* Lucy Mack Smith! Abrac is short for *Abracadabra,* and is a common, old-fashioned way of saying that they practiced magic."[1] "From early childhood he and his family had been dabbling in divination, necromancy, and various forms of ritual magic. Smith believed in and practiced occultism until his death. This is the secret foundation of the Mormon Church he established."[2]

Joseph Smith, Sr. bragged: **"I know more about money digging than any man in this generation, for I have been in the business more than thirty years."**[3] (Emphasis in the original)

The following is an account written by Fayette Lapham who had interviewed the Smith family around 1830:

> "This Joseph Smith, Senior, we soon learned, from his own lips, was a firm believer in witchcraft and other supernatural things; and had brought up his family in the same belief. He also believed that there was a vast amount of money buried somewhere in the country; that it would some day be found; that he himself had spent both time and money searching for it, with divining rods, but had not succeeded in finding any, though sure that he eventually would....

JOSEPH SMITH AND MAGIC

"His son Joseph,...happened to be where a man was looking into a dark stone and telling people, therefrom, where to dig for money and other things. Joseph requested the privilege of looking into the stone, which he did by **putting his face into the hat where the stone** was. It proved to be not the right stone for him; but he

could see some things, and, among them, he saw the stone, and where it was in which he could see whatever he wished to see....under pretense of digging a well, they found water and the stone at a depth of twenty or twenty-two feet. After this, Joseph spent about two years looking into this stone, telling fortunes, where to find lost things, and where to dig for money and other hidden treasure."[4] (Emphasis in the original)

We are also told that Joshua Stafford "became acquainted with the family of Joseph Smith, Sen. about the year 1819 or 20. They...told marvellous (sic) stories about ghosts, hobgoblins, caverns, and various other mysterious matters."[5]

NECROMANCY

"Joseph Smith himself practiced 'glass-looking,' a 19th century term for scrying or crystal-ball gazing....In fact, Joseph's annual meetings (on a witchcraft holiday) with the *angel* Moroni on hill Cumorah were actually attempts to conjure up a demon spirit through magic and necromancy. There is strong evidence that in 1824 he actually had *to dig up the body of his dead brother, Alvin,* and bring part of that body with him to the hill to gain the gold plates!

"Joseph Smith was also well-known in his community for using blood sacrifices in his magic rituals to find hidden treasure. One report said that:

"'Jo [sic] Smith the prophet, told my uncle William Stafford, he wanted a fat black sheep. He said that he wanted to cut its throat and make it walk in a circle three times around and it would prevent a pot of money from leaving.'"[6] (Emphasis in the original)

Smith also approved of another occult practice—that of divining with magic rods. He even referred to the "gift of working with the rod" in one of his revelations but later he falsified the revelation and removed the reference to the rod. The original statement said:

JOSEPH SMITH AND MAGIC

"Now this is not all, for you have another gift, which is the gift of **working with the rod:** behold it has told you things: behold there is no other power save God, that can cause this **rod of nature, to work in your hands,...**"

This passage was then changed to the following:

"Now this is not all thy gift; for you have another gift, which is the **gift of Aaron;** behold, it has told you many things;

"Behold, there is no other power, save the power of God, that can cause this **gift of Aaron to be with you.**"[7] (Emphasis in the original)

THE DIVINING ROD (DOWSING)

What is interesting to note is that the "Rod of Aaron" is just another name for the Caduceus or the divining rod in occult terminology![8] (For more information on dowsing or the divining rod, see my article entitled "Dowsing Is in the Bible," which is available from Sharing. See listing in the back of the book.)

On July 28, 1971, Wesley P. Walters and Fred Poffarl discovered a box in a basement storage room beneath Chenango County jail which contained the "...records of Judge Albert Neely and Constable Philip M. DeZeng. These proved once and for all that Joseph Smith had indeed been arrested and found guilty on March 20, 1826, of pretending to find buried treasure by 'glass-looking.'"[9]

This "1826 trial proves beyond all doubt that Joseph Smith used a stone which he placed in his hat to try to locate buried treasures. This was, of course, a common practice by magicians and individuals influenced by the occult."[10]

It appears as though Smith believed that guardians protected hidden treasures. One person wondered if these guardian spirits could have been transformed by Joseph into the angel which supposedly appeared to him and gave him the golden plates. Fayette Lapham interviewed Joseph, Sr. and wrote the following about Joseph, Jr. She said that he:

> "...told his father that, in his dream, a very large and tall man appeared to him, dressed in an ancient suit of clothes, and the clothes were bloody. And the man said to him that there was a valuable treasure, buried many years since, and not far from that place; and that he had now arrived for it to be brought to light, for the benefit of the world at large; and, if he would strictly follow his directions, he would direct him to the place where it was deposited, in such a manner that he could obtain it....and one dark night, Joseph...arrived at a large boulder, of several tons weight, when he was immediately impressed with the idea that the object of his pursuit was under that rock."[11]

UNSUCCESSFUL ATTEMPT

After unsuccessfully trying to obtain the treasure and having the rock slide back into place, he was struck with such force that he ended up on his back.

Lapham continues:

> "As he lay there, he looked up and saw the same large man that had appeared in his dream, dressed in the same clothes. He said to him that, when the treasure was deposited there, he **was sworn to take charge of and protect that property,** until the time should arrive for it to be exhibited to the world of mankind; and, in order to prevent his making an improper disclosure, **he was murdered or slain on the spot, and the treasure**

had been under his charge ever since. He said to him that he had not followed his directions; and, in consequence of laying the article down before putting it in the napkin, he could not have the ar[t]cle (sic) now; but that if he would come again, one year from that time, he could have them."[12] (Emphasis in the original)

Isn't this reminiscent of Smith's version of how he obtained the plates in the first place? Remember that when Joseph tried to withdraw the gold plates, Moroni appeared to him and forbade him to do so. This messenger told him that he was unable to remove these plates for four more years but that he should come back to this place in precisely one year. Eventually the plates were delivered to him. Is there a connection? Was Joseph's story really based on this occult phenomenon?

In fact, Joseph and Heil Lewis, Joseph Smith's wife's cousins:

"...recalled hearing Joseph tell that he had learned 'by a dream' the location of the buried gold plates, and having gone to dig them up had been confronted by a ghost that looked 'like a Spaniard having a long beard... with his throat cut from ear to ear, and the blood streaming down' who told him how to obtain the release of the plates from the enchantment that held them."[13]

WHY DOES MASONRY ENTER IN?

Martin Harris, one of the "witnesses" to the *Book of Mormon,* stated: "While on his way home with the plates, he was met by **what appeared to be a man,** who demanded the plates, and struck him with a club on his side, which was all black and blue."[14] (Emphasis in the original)

This reference reminds me of the story of Hiram Abiff in Masonry. Hiram Abiff was also accosted by three ruffians who end up striking the candidate (who is representing Hiram Abiff). The last blow takes Hiram Abiff's life. Smith would have been familiar with this legend for a reason that will be disclosed later.

But this is not the end of Joseph Smith's fascination with the occult.

> "[A]fter his death, Smith was found to be carrying a magic talisman on his person sacred to Jupiter, and designed to bring him power and success in seducing women."[15] (Emphasis in the original)

JOSEPH SMITH'S TALISMAN

A lengthy quotation from a Mormon will give insight into this aspect. Dr. Reed Durham was the Director of the LDS Institute of Religion at the University of Utah when he gave a presidential address to the Mormon History Association on April 20, 1974. This admission almost cost him his church membership. He said:

> "...I should like to initiate all of you into what is perhaps the strangest, the most mysterious, occult-like esoteric, and yet Masonically oriented practice ever adopted by Joseph Smith....

> "All available evidence suggests that **Joseph Smith the Prophet possessed a magical Masonic medallion,** or talisman, which he worked during his lifetime and which was evidently on his person when he was martyred....

> "...purchased from Emma Smith Bidamon family, fully notarized by that family to be authentic and to have belonged to Joseph Smith, [it—D.H. & E.D.] can now be identified as a **Jupiter talisman.** It carries the sign

JOSEPH SMITH AND MAGIC

and image of Jupiter and...in some very...mysterious sense...[it—D.H. & E.D.] was the appropriate talisman for Joseph Smith to possess.

"I wasn't able to find what this was...[until—D.H. & E.D.] finally in a **magic** book printed in England in 1801...how thrilled I was when I saw in his list of magic seals the very talisman which Joseph Smith had in his possession at the time of his martyrdom....

"In astrology, Jupiter is always associated with high positions, getting one's own way....So closely is magic bound up with the stars and astrology that the term astrologer and magician were in ancient times almost synonymous.

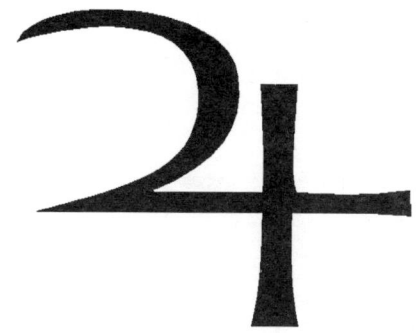

"The purpose of the Table of Jupiter in talismanic magic was to be able to call upon the celestial intelligences, assigned to the particular talisman, to assist one in all endeavors. The names of the deities which...could be invoked...were always written on the talisman...three such names were written on Joseph Smith's talisman....

"When properly invoked, with Jupiter being very powerful and ruling in the heavens, these intelligences—by the power of ancient magic—guaranteed to the possessor of this talisman the gain of riches and favor and power and love and peace...and anyone who worked skillfully with this Jupiter Table would obtain the power of stimulating anyone to offer his love to the possessor of the talisman, whether from a friend, brother, relative, or even any female."[16]

MARTYR OR MURDERER?

So Smith was involved in occult practices right up to his death. Of course, the Mormons feel that Smith was a martyr, but that is not really the case. The Mormons had moved to Nauvoo, Illinois by 1839.

> "Soon the local newspaper, the *Nauvoo Expositor*, began to criticize the Mormons—for their belief in polygamy among other things. The Mormon 'Legion' destroyed the newspaper office, and Smith was arrested. On June 27, 1844, an angry mob stormed the jail. Smith was shot and Mormonism had its first martyr."[17]

What Mormon accounts fail to tell the public is that Joseph had in his possession a six-shooter. The rest of the story is that:

> "Joseph was in the second floor of the jail, with visiting friends and without a locked door. After members of his own militia retired to their homes for the night, a mob formed outside, shouting insults. As some of the mob came up the narrow stairwell, Joseph discharged his pistol into their midst, killing 2 men and wounding a third. He and his brother, Hyrum, were killed in the exchange of gunfire.
>
> "Under no circumstance can Joseph Smith be described as a martyr, sealing his testimony of the Book of Mormon with blood. He died in a gunfight, in a tragic ending caused by his own carnal, sinful use of other men's wives."[18]

WHO IS MORMO?

Knowing of Smith's penchant for the occult, I think it is quite interesting that he chose the name "Mormon" for his group. You see, in *The Satanic Bible,* the name "Mormo" is listed as one of the "infernal names" of Satan.[19] Logically, a follower of Mormo could be called a Mormon!

In *Meet the Vampire* we find:

> "In ancient Greece and Rome, there were several types of monsters or ghosts that could be called vampires. Best known was the lamia, who sometimes appeared as a beautiful woman and sometimes as a woman whose lower body looked like a snake. Lamias (or lamiae) either ate their victims or sucked their blood, like true vampires. They also had the horrid ability to take their eyes out of their heads. One particular lamia was named **Mormo.**

Roman mothers used to frighten their children with her name."[20]

Mormo is also listed as the "King of the Ghouls, consort of Hecate."[21] Hecate was the Goddess of the Dark of the Moon, the black nights when the moon is hidden. She was associated with the **deeds of darkness,** the Goddess of the Crossways, which were held to be **ghostly places of evil magic.**[22]

Laurie Cabot, a witch, states: "At death Hecate was said to meet the departed souls and lead them to the Underworld....And so Hecate became known as the Queen of the Witches...."[23]

It's no wonder, then, that Hecate is called the "Queen of the Witches" since she taught **SORCERY** and **WITCHCRAFT.**[24]

Don't the characteristics of Hecate fit quite well with Joseph Smith's belief in magic and guardian spirits, etc.?

Concerning familiar spirits, Mormon Apostle LeGrand Richards wrote a book defending Mormonism in which he stated:

> "Their speech would be low out of the dust; their voice would be as one that hath a familiar spirit, out of the ground; their speech would whisper out of the dust. Now, obviously, the only way a dead people could speak 'out of the ground' or 'low out of the dust' would be by the written word, and this the people did **through the Book of Mormon. Truly it has a familiar spirit,** for it contains the words of the prophets of the God of Israel."[25]

Here is an admission from one of the Mormon Apostles that the *Book of Mormon* has a familiar spirit! Could Smith's involvement with the spirit world account for the Mormon doctrine of baptism for the dead?

Of course, since Joseph Smith's habit of playing with the occult has come to light, some Mormon scholars are now trying to justify his practices. For instance, some scholars said:

> "...that he wasn't any worse than anybody else living at that time because belief in and practice of magic was pervasive in the 18th and early 19th century America.
>
> "The scholars go on to say that it was the coming of the enlightenment and rationalism that changed people's outlook on occult practices. These scholars say that since we don't live in that culture any longer, it's hard for us to put ourselves in those people's shoes.
>
> "However, research shows that as early as 1788 in New York, and equally as early in Vermont, there were laws against occult practices such as palmistry and witchcraft and that the press was generally unfavorable to such claims."[26]

In the next chapter we will look at Mormonism and godhood (which was Satan's lie to Eve) and also show many similarities between Mormonism and Masonry. Remember, however, even if Mormonism tries to justify occult practices, the Bible explicitly warns us:

> "There shall not be found among you **any one** that maketh his son or his daughter to pass through the fire, or that **useth divination, or an observer of times,** or an enchanter, or a witch, Or a charmer, **or a consulter with familiar spirits,** or a wizard, **or a necromancer.** For **all** that do these things are an **abomination** unto the LORD..." (Deuteronomy 18:10-12).

Chapter Four

MORMONISM AND GODHOOD

The idea of godhood is an integral part of Mormonism. In fact, the promise of man one day becoming a god has an attraction to many people. One Mormon booklet states: "Life is purposeful. It is progressive. **IT LEADS TO GODHOOD.**"[1] The *Doctrine and Covenants,* one of the Mormon "scriptures," declares: "Then shall they be gods."[2] James Talmage, a Mormon Elder, stated: "In spite of the opposition of the sects, in the face of direct charges of blasphemy, the [Mormon] Church proclaims the eternal truth: **'AS MAN IS, GOD ONCE WAS; AS GOD IS, MAN MAY BE.'**"[3] Brigham Young claimed: "The Lord created you and me for the purpose of **BECOMING GODS LIKE HIMSELF....**We are created, **we are born...to BECOME GODS** like unto our Father in heaven."[4] He also said: "Man is the king of kings and lord of lords in embryo" and "Gods exist, and we had better strive to be prepared to be one of them."[5]

Joseph Smith announced:

> "God himself was once as we are now, and is an exalted man, and sits enthroned in yonder heavens!... Here then is eternal life—to know the only wise and true God; and you have got to learn how to be gods yourselves, and to be kings and priests to God, the same as all gods have done before you, namely, by going from one small degree to another, and from a small capacity to a great one; from grace to grace, from exaltation to

exaltation, until you attain to the resurrection of the dead, and are able to dwell in everlasting burnings...."[6]

The sad part is that they will dwell in "everlasting burnings," but that place is called hell, not heaven.

LeGrand Richards, however, hastens to remind us that "it will be seen that **MEN CAN BECOME GODS...only by observing the new and everlasting covenant of marriage,** and that without marriage they can only become 'ministering servants [angels]....'"[7] We can see by this statement that one must be married before being able to attain godhood. Ora Pate Stewart comments:

> "There was a Mother, too, but she is included in the title God. He could never have achieved Godhood, let alone Eternal Fatherhood, without a glorified helpmate. It is the hope of achieving this divine relationship that makes marriage such a holy contract. As God is, man may become. **But he cannot become as God without a wife. That is why we marry for time and eternity.**"[8]

Looking into the Bible, however, we find that Paul writes: "Art thou bound unto a wife? seek not to be loosed. Art thou loosed from a wife? Seek not a wife....So then he that giveth her in marriage doeth well; but he that giveth her not in marriage doeth better" (I Corinthians 7:27, 38). Either Paul was ignorant of Mormon doctrine or the Mormons are unscriptural in their claims. In spite of all these discrepancies Mormons still claim that Mormon doctrine and Bible doctrine are one and the same!

CONTRADICTORY INSTRUCTIONS

Mormons also believe that when God placed Adam and Eve in the Garden of Eden that He gave them contradictory instructions. God told them not to touch the tree of the knowledge of good and evil and at the same time He said that they should be fruitful and multiply. Mormons claim that Adam and Eve could not be fruitful and multiply **UNLESS** they partook of this forbidden tree so they were forced to choose between eating of the tree of the knowledge of good and evil or remaining fruitless. Of course, Adam and Eve made the correct choice when they decided to disobey God—at least according to Mormon theology.

Another one of the Mormon "scriptures," the *Pearl of Great Price,* says:

> "And in that day Adam blessed God and was filled, and began to prophesy concerning all the families of the earth, saying: Blessed be the name of God, for BECAUSE OF MY TRANSGRESSION MY EYES ARE OPENED, and in this life I shall have joy, and again in the flesh I shall see God. And Eve, his wife, heard all these things and was glad, saying: WERE IT NOT FOR OUR TRANSGRESSION we never should have had seed, and never should have known good and evil, and the joy of our redemption, and the eternal life which God giveth unto all the obedient (Moses 5:10-11)."

The *Book of Mormon* states in II Nephi 2:25: "Adam fell that men might be; and men are, that they might have joy." The Bible, on the other hand, tells us that "the way of transgressors is hard" (Proverbs 13:15), not joyful. Genesis 3:16-17 also gives us the result of Adam's and Eve's transgression:

> "Unto the woman He [God] said, I will greatly multiply thy SORROW and thy conception; in SORROW thou shalt bring forth children....And unto Adam He said, Because thou hast hearkened unto the voice of thy wife, and hast eaten of the tree, of which I commanded thee, saying, Thou shalt not eat of it:

MORMONISM AND GODHOOD 69

CURSED is the ground for thy sake; in SORROW shalt thou eat of it all the days of thy life...."

Does this sound like a joyful situation?

Mormon Eldon Hicks writes: "The fall of Adam and Eve was a NECESSARY change...in order to provide mortal parentage for the spirit children of God who were ready and waiting for the experience of earth life."[9] In other words, Adam's fall allowed these obedient, heavenly spirit beings to come to earth and to inhabit an earthly body. Had Adam not fallen, these spirits would not have been privileged to be born here on earth. Mormon doctrine teaches:

"...that every one of us existed before we were born. Our spirits were conceived in this 'pre-existence' by a physical act of God with one of His heavenly wives. The Mormons sing:

In the heav'ns are parents single?
No! The tho't makes reason stare!
Truth is reason; truth eternal
Tells me I've a mother there."[10]

Of course, there is no such teaching in the Bible.

SPECIAL UNDERGARMENTS

The creation story is presented in motion picture form as part of the endowment ceremony.[11] Only about 30% of the Mormon membership have gone through this endowment ceremony. Those who have received their endowments should now be wearing a special undergarment which is knee-length and has short cap sleeves. There are Masonic markings of a compass on the left breast and a square on the right breast. Also, the navel mark and the right knee mark consist of a small slash. In the early days of Mormonism the slashes were cut into the garment while it was on the person, actually drawing blood. This blood "sealed" the oaths that later took place during the temple ceremony. (The Bible warns us not to make any cuttings in our flesh [Deuteronomy 14:1], yet the Mormons at one time also went against this injunction.)

This garment is to be worn at all times (and Mormons are even buried in it) and acts as a **magical talisman** to the Mormon as it is supposed to protect him or her from Satan. When the garment wears out, the markings are cut out and then burned. After this, it doesn't matter what happens to the garment. This proves that the "magic" is in the markings, not the garment itself. A new name is also given with this garment. Mormons believe that they will be called forth on the resurrection morning by this new name that they have received.

In *The God Makers* we find an interesting incident. When former Mormon, Ed Decker, was on a speaking tour in Brazil, he:

> "...dressed himself in the Mormon Temple costume to show his audience what it looked like, unaware of the effect it would have. When he came out on the stage of the large auditorium, the audience took one frightened look at him and panicked. There was a great commotion, as though someone had yelled 'Fire!' That was how he learned that the high priests of the satanic Macumba [voodoo/Santeria] cult wear white costumes almost identical to Mormon Temple clothing, including the peculiar white hat and unique robes of Joseph Smith's Melchizedek or High Priesthood."[12]

SATAN WEARS MASONIC APRON

At this point I would like to briefly discuss parts of what is shown to the patrons (those members who are partaking of this endowment ceremony) in the temple. The movie opens up with the voices of Elohim (the Mormon God), Jehovah, and the Archangel Michael, who eventually is created as Adam. Michael, who had attained godhood on another planet, became Adam on this earth and Eve had been ONE of his wives. While Adam and Eve are in the Garden they receive a visitor, Satan, who is wearing an apron with Masonic markings on it. This apron is of a dark blue color, representing the higher degrees of Masonry. Adam asks Satan what is on his apron and he replies that it is an emblem of his power and priesthood. Satan then tries to entice Adam to partake of the fruit of the forbidden tree. When Adam refuses, Satan approaches Eve. Eve queries: "Who are you?" and he replies: "I am your brother." (Mormons actually believe that Satan [Lucifer] is our brother.) Eve explains that she doesn't want to eat of this tree because God has forbidden her to do so. Satan says: "Ye shall not surely die." Eve then asks if there is any other way and he answers that there is no other way out, so Eve does eat of the fruit of the tree.

It is now time for Elohim and Jehovah to check on Adam (the former Archangel Michael) and Eve, so Satan tells them that they should make an apron of fig leaves and hide quickly so that Elohim will not see their nakedness. Adam and Eve then make their aprons and wear them throughout the remainder of the movie. Also, at this point, each patron pulls out a green satin fig leaf apron and puts it on and continues to wear it throughout the rest of the ceremony. What is strange is that the undergarment that God supposedly wants the patrons to wear throughout their entire lives is under their other clothing. However, the apron that Satan tells them to wear is put on top of their other clothing. It seems that Satan's suggested garment is more important to the Mormons than the one that they believe God told them to wear. This fig leaf apron is even worn when the Mormons are married.

WHO IS THE GOD OF MORMONISM?

After Adam and Eve are expelled from Eden (according to Mormon belief), Adam erects an altar and offers the following prayer: "Oh, God, hear the words of my mouth. Oh, God, hear the words of my mouth. Oh, God, hear the words of my mouth." After he is done uttering his prayer, Satan (Lucifer) answers him by replying: "I hear you. What is it you want?" Adam asks Satan who he is and he replies that he is the god of this world. Isn't it strange that Satan answers Adam's prayer when Adam is supposed to be praying to God? Doesn't this make it quite evident who the Mormon god is?

Originally the words to Adam's prayer were claimed to be spoken in the so-called Adamic language and were said to be "Pay lay ale. Pay lay ale. Pay lay ale." If you would take *Strong's Exhaustive Concordance* and look up these words in the Hebrew language you would find that "Pele" (Pay lay) (p. 94, #6382) means "wonderful" and that "Heylel" (ale) (p. 32, #1966) means "Lucifer"! Was Adam actually praying to "Wonderful Lucifer?" It would not be surprising because it is Lucifer who responds to Adam's prayer by saying: "I hear you. What is it you want?" Masons (and other New Agers) revere Lucifer and there are many similarities between Masonry and Mormonism, so it is quite possible (and most likely probable) that Adam was praying to Lucifer in this Mormon creation movie.[13]

During this ceremony, the patron must perform the Five Points of Fellowship. This is identical to Masonry. This position is: foot to foot, knee to knee, chest to chest, hand to back, and mouth to ear. In this position, the patron chants: "Health in the navel, marrow in the bones, strength in the loins and in the sinews, power in the Priesthood be upon me and upon my posterity through all generations of time and throughout all eternity!"[14]

Former Mormon, Ed Decker, states:

"Of course, this is a classic form of occultic incantation and was in use in witchcraft and Satan worship long before the Mormon Temple Ceremony came about, and is reportedly recorded in the notorious 'Grimorum Verum' kept by druidic priests and warlocks. What is frightening is the calling down of the Luciferian priesthood or priestcraft upon the patron and the patron's family for future generations, a curse that must be broken by the power of the true God!"[15, 16]

WITCHCRAFT'S FIVEFOLD KISS

What is interesting is that in witchcraft there is a "Fivefold Kiss" that very closely resembles the "Five Points of Fellowship." One difference is that each point (the feet, knees, phallus, breasts, and mouth) is actually kissed in witchcraft.[17]

The Great Rite (ritual sexual intercourse) is practiced in witchcraft. A ritual written by Aleister Crowley, a Satanist and Mason, says:

> "Open for me the secret way:
> The pathway of Intelligence
> Between the gates of night and day,
> Beyond the boundaries of time and sense.
>
> "Behold the Mystery aright.
> **The Five Points of Fellowship,**
> Here where Lance and Grail unite,
> And feet and knees and breasts and lips."[18]

One former Mormon, Mason, witch, and Satanist remarked: "We were told that in doing this, we were joining an ancient, 'apostolic succession' of high priesthood authority, which could be traced all the way back to Jesus and his 'high priestess,' Mary Magdelene."[19] Again, you can see some of the blasphemous aspects of the occult.

Can you see the connection between the priesthood of witchcraft, and that of Mormonism and Masonry? In Alex Horne's Masonic book, *King Solomon's Temple in the Masonic Tradition,* is this amazing admission: "'We would suggest,

MORMONISM AND GODHOOD

though only tentatively,' Knoop and Jones say, in comment, 'that the **five points of fellowship may have originated in practices connected with witchcraft** or some other superstition, of which there was then no lack in Scotland.'"[20]

MORMONISM AND MASONRY

Does it come as a shock to you that there are similarities between Mormonism and Masonry? If you would study both religions you could easily see the resemblances for yourself. You see, Joseph Smith, the founder of Mormonism, was a Mason. Other prominent Mormons who were also Masons were Hyrum Smith, Brigham Young, Heber C. Kimball, and John C. Bennett.[21]

Ed Decker, a former Mormon, explains:

"In the early days of the Mormon Church, Joseph Smith and several other Mormon leaders organized the first Masonic Lodge in Nauvoo, Illinois.

"Joseph Smith was initiated into Masonry on March 15, 1842—and the very next day was elevated to the 32nd degree sublime Master of the Royal Secret!

"This so irritated the Masonic hierarchy that they revoked the charter. About 1500 Mormons were kicked out of Masonry at that time.

"Almost immediately thereafter, the Temple Ceremony of Mormonism came into effect. It coincides with Masonic ritual in several dozen specific places.

"Here are a few of the symbols and rites that are common to both Masonic Lodge ritual and Mormon Temple ceremonies: the all-seeing eye, the anointing of oil, the wearing of an apron, the beehive, the compass,

the earth, the emblem of the clasped hands, the five points of fellowship, the special garment and garment markings, the special grips and handshakes, the continual use of the expression 'holiness to the Lord', the moon symbol, a new name given, secrets revealed, levels of priesthood, use of the square, star and sun symbols; penalties agreed to under blood oaths, etc."[22]

SAME OATHS AS MASONS RECEIVE

During the temple ceremony Mormons are given names, signs, and penalties which they are not allowed to divulge, even at the peril of their own lives. Mormons believe that they will be tested on these secret laws, signs, and tokens before being allowed to enter into heaven. The Mormon penalty for revealing the secret handclasp of the first token of the Aaronic Priesthood to anyone else was at one time described as "having your throat slit from ear to ear and your tongue torn out by the roots." The penalty for revealing the second token of the Aaronic Priesthood was described as having "your chest cut open and your heart and vitals torn out and fed to the beasts of the field and the fowl of the air." The final penalty is for the first token of the Melchizedek Priesthood and was worded as "having your body cut asunder and your vitals and bowels gush out upon the ground." Because of complaints, however, the wording has now been changed to state "various ways in which

life can be taken." The same type blood oaths are found in Masonry.

"The Grand Lodge F. & A.M. of Utah, has published a book written by S.H. Goodwin, P.G.M. and former Grand Secretary. This book gives the Mormon oaths, signs, and grips and declares: 'The observant Craftsman [Mason—F.S.] cannot be long among the Mormon people without noting the not-infrequent use made of certain emblems and symbols which have come to be associated in the public mind with the Masonic fraternity....He will sometimes be made aware of the fact, when shaking hands with a Mormon neighbor, or friend, that there is a pressure of the hand as though some sort of "grip" is being given.' He adds: 'Joseph Smith fixed the date of the introduction of the endowments [the secret work in Mormon temples—F.S.] as May 4, 1842, nearly two month (sic) after he became a Mason.'"[23]

The apron that I mentioned earlier is also very important to the Masonic tradition. Masonic writer, W. L. Wilmshurst, states: "Brethren, I charge you to regard your APRON as one of the MOST PRECIOUS and speaking symbols our Order [Masonry] has to give you."[24, 25] However, these aprons were not satisfactory to God for He made coats to clothe Adam and Eve (Genesis 3:7, 21). Yet Mormonism and Masonry prefer the aprons to the clothing provided by God.

LEVELS OF PRIESTHOOD

Another similarity between Mormonism and Masonry is the levels of priesthood. Both groups have a Melchizedek Priesthood. Mormon LeGrand Richards tells us: "Before a man can receive the blessings of eternal marriage, he must be ordained an elder in the Melchizedek Priesthood...."[26] He also states: "It is evident, therefore, that a man must receive the priesthood after the order of Melchizedek to qualify for exaltation [godhood] in the celestial kingdom."[27] So, to become a god, according to Mormon doctrine, one must belong to the Melchizedek Priesthood. Masonry also has a Melchizedek Priesthood. The 19th degree of Scottish Rite Masonry is called "Grand Pontiff." It is during this ceremony that the "Candidate is anointed with oil, is made and proclaimed a priest for ever according to the Order of Melchizedek." Hebrews 5:5, 9 tells us, however, that "Christ glorified not Himself to be made an high priest" but was "called OF GOD an high priest after the order of Melchizedek," but Mormons and Masons glorify THEMSELVES and take ON THEMSELVES the honor of priesthood that was given to Christ ALONE.

Mormons not only try to take a priesthood that was given to Christ alone, but they also take upon themselves the Aaronic priesthood which could only be given to those of the tribe of Levi, but not just anyone from the tribe of Levi could be a priest. It had to be a person whose lineage came through Aaron. The tribe of Levi was given to do the service of the tabernacle but the priesthood could only be held by those who came from Aaron's line. In Numbers 16 we find that Korah and others from the tribe of Levi confronted Moses and told him that he was taking too much upon himself, but Moses replied that they were taking too much upon themselves. He then asked them: "[S]eek ye the priesthood also?" (Numbers 16:10). The Lord then destroyed them because they were out of place in what they did. A warning follows in Numbers 16:40 that "no stranger, which is not of the seed of Aaron, come near to offer incense before the LORD; that he be not as Korah, and as his company...."

The Aaronic priesthood, however, was brought to an end by the death of Christ. Hebrews 7:11-12 states:

> "If therefore perfection were by the Levitical priesthood, (for under it the people received the law,) what further need was there that another priest should rise after the order of Melchisedec, and not be called after the order of Aaron? For the priesthood being changed, there is made of necessity a change also of the law."

This chapter then goes on to reveal that Christ "because He continueth ever, hath an **unchangeable priesthood**" (Hebrews 7:24). The word "unchangeable" is "aparabatos" in the Greek and means **"UNTRANSFERABLE."** In other words, this priesthood cannot be passed on from one person to another. Christ is the **one and only one** who can hold this priesthood.

MORMON'S GOD IS SATAN

In my book on Masonry, *Hidden Secrets of Masonry,* I show (with extensive documentation) that the Masons' "God" is actually Satan or Lucifer. We have also seen in this book on Mormonism how that (according to Mormonism) Adam prayed to "God" and Satan answered him. Since Mormonism and Masonry have so many things in common, is not Mormonism's "God" also Satan?

Chapter Five

PARALLELS BETWEEN MORMONISM AND MASONRY

W. J. McK. McCormick gives an extensive list of the parallels between Mormonism and Masonry. They are:

"1. Both have Temples.

2. First token of Aaronic Priesthood similar to E.A. [Entered Apprentice] Degree.

    A. Obligation to secrecy common to both.
    B. Penal sign (thumb to throat...) identical.
    C. Grip of E.A. and 1st token of Aaronic Priesthood similar.
    D. Similar wording in both: 'What is this?'

3. The second token of the Aaronic Priesthood similar to the F.C. [Fellow Craft] Degree.
    A. Promise of *secrecy* re the name, sign, grip or penalty, etc.
    B. Similar Penal Sign in both.
    C. Similar grip in both.
    D. Both receive a name:...The Name of the Pass-grip of F.C. Mason is Shibboleth.

4. First token of the Melchisedec Priesthood Similar to M.M. [Master Mason] Degree.

A. The promise of Mormonism resembles the oath of Masonry.

B. Penal Sign similar in both.

C. A 'name' is used in both: Mormonism, 'The Name of this Token is the Son, meaning the Son of God'; Masonry, the Name of the Pass Grip from the 2nd to 3rd Degree is Tubal Cain.

D. The Masonic 'Five Points of Fellowship' are given at the Veil in the Mormon Temple Ceremony.

5. Mormons and Masons both have a vow of 'chastity'....

6. Mormon 'Sign of the Nail' is similar to the Knights of Malta grip. 'The Grand Commander now explains the grip and word of a Knight of Malta. He says to candidate—"Thomas, reach hither thy finger, and feel the print of the nails..."' (Point of first finger forced into the palm of the hand)....

7. The oath of Vengeance in the degree Knight Kadosh resembles the oath of Vengeance taken in Mormon Temples prior to 1931.

8. Masons and Mormons both change clothing before ceremonies.

9. Masons and Mormons both use an APRON.

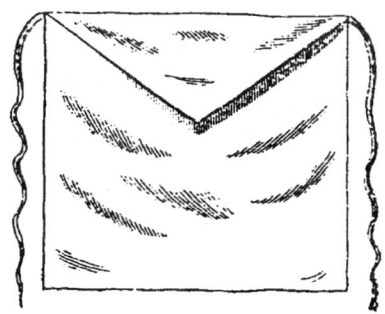

10. Masons in the 'higher degrees' anoint the candidate: Mormons do likewise.

11. Masons and Mormons receive a 'new name.'

12. Masons and Mormons both use 'Veils.'

13. Adam is personated in the Mormon Temple Ceremony and in 'Knights of the Sun' degree in masonry (sic).

14. God is personated in Mormon Temple Ceremony and in R.A. [Royal Arch] Degree of Masonry.

15. Masons use square and compasses. Mormons have the symbols of their 'sacred' garments and on the veil in the temple.

16. Mormons have the compass point marked over the left breast on the garment: Masons press the compass-point against the naked left breast.

17. The Mormon under-garment has the square marked on the right breast: Masons press the angle of the square against the right breast in their ritual.

18. Both Mormons and Masons use a mallet or common gavel...."[1]

Both Masonry and Mormonism also teach Satan's lie that "ye shall be as gods." This lie is one of the basic tenets of the NEW AGE MOVEMENT.[2] It is also interesting to know that Masons are looking for a "NEW AGE." Since Mormonism and Masonry have so many similarities and Masonry is part of the New Age Movement, could Mormonism also be involved with this movement? Well, a magazine put out by the Mormon Church for teenagers is called "THE NEW ERA." "Era," of course, is another word for "age," so in essence this magazine is called THE NEW AGE! Also, a number of years ago I received an empty packet of "Nutri Whey," one of Yurika Foods' products. On this package are these words: **"A NEW AGE PRODUCT."** What does this have to do with Mormonism? It's quite simple. You see, Yurika Foods is a MORMON-OWNED COMPANY! So, Mormonism is also PROMOTING the NEW AGE MOVEMENT through at least one of its products!

MORMON-OWNED COMPANIES

Another connection between the NEW AGE and Mormonism would be through one prominent Mormon, Cleon Skousen. Mr. Skousen was the former head of the F.B.I. and Founder and President of the Freeman Foundation which was founded in 1971. He also joined the faculty of the Brigham Young University. "Skousen was directed to start the Institute by former President of the Mormon Church, David O. McKay. In 1989 the name was changed to the *National Center for Constitutional Studies*. The goal is to bring in the religious and political kingdom of God under the Mormon prophet."[3]

Skousen spoke at the "God and Freedom Banquet" which was held in honor of Sun Myung Moon to welcome him home from prison. Cleon Skousen spoke very highly of Moon and said that God had sent "Rev." Moon to our country with a revelation and a message.

> "The Mormon/Moonie coalition involves the Freeman Institute's cooperation in a new global anti-communist crusade with CAUSA International, a Moonie front organization. Also involved in CAUSA are members of CARP (another of Moon's dozens of front groups), whose business cards read **'Pioneering New Leadership for the New Age.'** The Mormon Church has a great deal in common with the Unification Church."[4]

"CAUSA is of particular interest because its amazing ecumenism has brought together Moonies, Mormons, top military, scientific, and political figures, and the Christian Right in close cooperation to fight 'Communism.' Accompanied by leaders from his Freeman Institute, Dr. Skousen has been prominent at CAUSA Conferences. So have well-known Christian anticommunist crusaders. How can Mormons, Moonies, and Christians realistically work together? The Unification Church hopes to install Sun Myung Moon as world ruler; the Mormon Church holds the same ambition for its 'Prophet, Seer and Revelator'; and Christians await the return of Jesus Christ to establish His kingdom."[5]

"Much like Joseph Smith, Sun Myung Moon claims to have been visited by angels, Moses, Buddha,

and Jesus. Jesus allegedly gave Moon at age 16 the same assignment that Joseph Smith's 'God' from Kolob had already given him at the same age: to 'restore' true Christianity, beginning in the United States, and eventually to take over the entire world. Although the main characters are different, the basic Unification Church scenario, including blind obedience by members, is much the same as Mormonism's. Reminiscent of Joseph Smith, Sun Myung Moon says:

> "'I am your brain. Every people or every organization that goes against the Unification Church will gradually come down and die.'"[6]

MOON—A NEW AGE MESSIAH

Moon, by the way, is a NEW AGER and he also believes that he is the Messiah. So, here we have a very prominent Mormon OPENLY bragging up a NEW AGER and saying that God sent Moon to America with a message. The NEW AGE MOVEMENT certainly has more people and groups involved in it than most people will ever realize.

As just mentioned, the Freeman Institute was organized by the command of the former Mormon President and former F.B.I. head. Perhaps this is why *Time* magazine stated: "The FBI and CIA...have instituted Mormon-recruitment plans."[7] There are also: "Fifteen Mormon Senators and Representatives currently trek[king] the halls of Congress."[8]

Now let's look at some of the holdings of the Mormon church.

> "According to the *Arizona Republic,* the church collects at least $4.3 billion a year from its members, and another $400 million from its various enterprises....In Orlando, Florida, the Mormon cult owns 315,000 acres of land valued at $250 million. In March of this year [1994] they purchased KMEO-AM-FM in Phoenix for $12 million cash. The Mormons control at least 100 companies that generate about $400 million annually. An AP news article states that, 'The church's business

subsidiaries generate an additional $4 billion a year in sales, which, if counted in the total would make the Mormon Church an $8 billion-a-year corporation, comparable with Union Carbide and Borden Products.'"[9]

"The Mormon church is the second largest controlling shareholder in the Los Angeles *Times-Mirror* Corporation. The *Times-Mirror* owns: *Orange Coast Daily Pilot* (Costa Mesa, CA); *Newsday* (Long Island, NY); *Dallas Times Herald* (Dallas, TX); *The Hartford Currant* (Hartford, CT); *The Advocate* (Stanford, CT); *Greenwich Times* (Greenwich, CT); *Times; The Sporting News* (St. Louis, MO); *The Denver Post* (Denver, CO)."[10]

"According to the *Denver Post,* the Mormons own five insurance companies. Named among them is Beneficial Life Insurance which in turn owns shares in AT&T, Union Pacific, Ford, DuPont, Chrysler, General Motors, J.C. Penney, Nabisco, Shell Oil, IBM, Kodak, etc."[11]

THE LIST CONTINUES

"LDS church-farm-ranch system:

Meadow Fresh Farms was started by and is owned by Mormons. Also,

Deseret Ranch of Florida
Deseret Livestock Ranch
LDS Welfare Farms & Diaries
U&I, Inc.
Deseret Ranch of Canada
Elberta Farms
Various farm investments
Deseret Farms of Texas
Deseret Farms of California

> Templeview Farms
> Total Acreage—928,000"[12]

A few other Mormon-owned companies are: Ideal Corporation; Brite Music; Eagle Marketing; and several radio and TV stations.[13]

> "Marriott, the Mormon hotel man who is America's biggest seller of alcoholic beverages...also owns other businesses. Among them: Hot Shoppes, Roy Rogers and Farrell's Ice Cream Parlours....

> "According to *The Flaming Torch,* 'Marriott Hotel will continue selling porno movies because the money is good.'"[14]

The August 4th issue of *Time* also had some interesting facts about Mormon wealth:

> "The top beef ranch in the world is not the King Ranch in Texas. It is the Deseret Cattle & Citrus Ranch outside Orlando, Fla. It covers 312,000 acres; its value as real estate alone is estimated at $858 million. It is owned entirely by the Mormons. The largest producer of nuts in America, AgReserves, Inc., in Salt Lake City, is Mormon-owned. So are the Bonneville International Corp., the country's 14th largest radio chain, and the Beneficial Life Insurance Co., with assets of $1.6 billion. There are richer churches than the one based in Salt Lake City: Roman Catholic holdings dwarf Mormon wealth. But the Catholic Church has 45 times as many members. **There is no major church in the U.S. as active as the Latter-day Saints in economic life, nor, per capita, as successful at it....**

> "Besides the Bonneville International chain and Beneficial Life, the church owns a 52% holding in ZCMI, Utah's largest department-store chain....

"In the first century of corporate Mormonism, the church's leaders were partners, officers or directors in more than 900 Utah-area businesses. They owned woolen mills, cotton factories, 500 local co-ops, 150 stores and 200 miles of railroad. Moreover, when occasionally faced with competition they insisted that church members patronize LDS-owned businesses."[15]

"The **Hotel Temple Square Co.** owns much of the real estate around the headquarters in downtown Salt Lake City. Their **Polynesian Cultural Center** is Hawaii's No. 1 paid visitor attraction, with annual revenues of at least **$40 million....**

"The church owns **16 radio stations** and **one TV station.** 1996 sales: **$172 million.** *Deseret News* circulation: 65,000. **Deseret Book Co.** owns a chain of about 30 bookstores in Utah."[16] (Emphasis in the original)

FAMILY-ORIENTED?

The Mormons try to give the public impression that they are family-oriented. However, Norman and Muriel Hancock, fifth generation Mormons, don't think so. Norman's great-great-grandfather knew Joseph Smith and was one of the earliest followers of Mormonism, but the Hancocks no longer agree with Mormon doctrine. So, when their youngest son got married on May 10, 1990, they were barred from witnessing the ceremony in the Arizona Temple. In fact, they aren't the only parents who have had to wait outside during the ceremony.

"Temple rules permit only adult Mormons in good standing in the church and those who hold 'temple recommends' from their own bishops to enter any of its 43 [now 51] temples around the world. Inside, 'eternal ordinances' and endowments are performed, including marriages, or 'sealing ceremonies,' and rituals of baptism for the dead."

PARALLELS BETWEEN MORMONISM & MASONRY 91

Mr. Hancock states:

> "The Mormons spend millions to tell us all that they are a family-oriented organization in the ads they run every day on TV, but they aren't because I see evidence where they split families....
>
> "It's just difficult for me to have somebody tell me what I have to do to go see my kids married...."[17]

Mrs. Hancock said: "You bring a child into the world... and you want to get there at some of the most important events. Marriage is one of them. And, of course, it hurts when you can't be there."[18]

> "Non-Mormon relatives and friends and those Mormons whose standing in a church is not good enough for a 'temple recommend' typically attend only a reception sometime after the ceremony."[19]

Of course the Mormons try to give an even greater impression that they are decent and good-living people. They are supposed to avoid alcoholic beverages, tobacco, and even caffeine, yet the Mormon-owned Marriott Hotel is the largest seller of alcoholic beverages and pornographic movies! Also, when the statistics are studied, some interesting facts are revealed. For instance, from the February 23, 1992 issue of the *Salt Lake Tribune* we discover that:

> *"The percentage of Utah's young adults who have tried amphetamines, sedatives, tranquilizers and pain medications is considerably higher than national averages. But even more disturbing is the finding that regular drug use among Utah adults 18-25 does **not** reflect the downward trend seen in this age group nationally."*[20] (Emphasis in the original.)

> "Tobacco use among the same Utah group jumped 51% from 1979 to 1989! The abuse of pain medications

has more than doubled, and the abuse of sedatives has more than quadrupled in the same period."[21]

FORMER MORMON CONFESSES

Lloyd C. Button, a former Mormon, confesses:

"We hear so much of the fact that Mormons do not drink coffee, tea, or liquor, and live such clean lives. May I say this, that our church had a large auditorium which was used frequently for dances on Saturday evenings. I witnessed things at those dances that differs greatly from the public image that is currently held of Mormon conduct....I saw as much drunkenness on those Saturday nights as in many other places, and just as many off-colored stories were heard as well....

"I'm sorry to say that it was drink that lead my mother to divorce my Mormon father. The drinking parties in my home were attended by so-called 'good' Mormons. So you can see why I'm a bit upset when I hear non-Mormons comment on the goodness of the Mormons, as if just being a Mormon was a guarantee of good conduct; I lived too long in a Mormon community to believe that."[22]

The Arizona Daily Star discloses:

"Pari-mutuel betting [gambling] was briefly legalized in Utah in 1925 and has some fans within the Mormon Church. The winter 1989 edition of Utah

Historical Quarterly contains a photograph depicting Mormon Church President Heber J. Grant and Gov. George Dern at a horse race.

"Grant's brother, Brigham S. Grant, then general manager of the church-owned Deseret News, briefly chaired the state's racing commission."[23]

"The **Salt Lake Tribune** reports that suicide is 'Utah's 8th leading cause of death' (July 14, 1991, pg. B-1). An accompanying chart shows that Utah's suicide rate is 23.2 per 1,000 for males and 7.2 per 1,000 for females, which gives it the sixth highest figures in the nation. The national average is 22.5 per 1,000 for males and 5.4 per 1,000 for females.

"These figures, though tragic, would be unremarkable were it not for Mormon claims. Their ads invariably depict the members of the church as happy, well-adjusted family members. Several times the claim has been made that Mormons are superior to other people. If this were indeed the case, we should not be seeing such high rates of suicide in a state that is 77.2 percent LDS."[24]

By 1995 "Utah rank[ed] fifth in the nation for suicides among 12 to 19-year-olds with a record 44 suicides in that age group...."[25]

Yet another brochure states:

"In Utah, a state in which Mormons predominate, conditions exist that would not suggest this high degree of moral character. For nearly 20 years, Utah has had the nation's highest divorce rate. It has ranked first in fraud schemes, has ranked high in teen pregnancies and teen suicides, and maintained a high crime rate. Salt Lake City, home of the LDS headquarters, currently is faced with a growing homosexual community and has at least a half-dozen gay bars. Statistics also indicate that Salt Lake City also has an increasing number of female alcoholics."[26]

CHILD ABUSE

The Evangel, quoting from an August 10, 1991 article in the *Salt Lake Tribune,* informs us:

"'Utah ranks second in the nation for reported incidents of child sexual abuse per capita,' executive director Carlos Y. Robey of the Intermountain Sexual Abuse Treatment Center stated.

"He reported, 'Child abusers are spread across the entire socioeconomic spectrum and leaders at every church level.'

"'There are abusing bishops, stake presidents, elders, quorum presidents, and Boy Scout leaders throughout this valley.'

"The article indicated that LDS leaders often testify in court **on behalf of the abuser.**"[27]

In fact, the wonderful "family" image is shattered by the following report: "General Relief Society President Elaine Jack said **ONLY 19 PERCENT OF CHURCH MEMBERS LIVE IN TRADITIONAL HOUSEHOLDS** with a mother, father and children...."[28]

Obviously, not only is Mormonism not what it is bragged up to be, but Mormonism has one doctrine after another that is contrary to God's Word, there is a close connection to the occultic Masonic organization, and at least one of its affiliations is connected with the NEW AGE MOVEMENT.

CONTRADICTIONS

Mormonism even contradicts itself in many areas and in trying to prove that they are the true church, they have proven that they are not the true church! For instance, Mormonism claims that there are 17 requirements to prove that a church is authentic. They maintain that they are the only ones who meet all of these requirements.[29]

One of these requirements is that "The true church must bear the name of Jesus Christ." Former Mormon, Bill Schnoebelen, states:

> "The name of the church at its founding in 1830 was the Church of Christ. In 1834, the church's name was **CHANGED** to the Church of the Latter-day Saints! No mention of Jesus in the title now. This remained the name of the church for four more years, until 1838, when it was changed finally to the Church of Jesus Christ of Latter-day Saints."[30] (Emphasis in the original)

So, the "true church" according to Mormonism did not meet the requirement of the "true church."

Another requirement is that the true church cannot have a paid ministry. But, Mormonism once again does not meet its own requirements.

> "Ward officials work for free but regional and general authorities of the Church are paid. These salaries are modest; but you must add that the general authorities sit on the boards of huge corporations which the Church owns. The last reported income of a member of the First Presidency was in the 6 figure bracket; and most of that came as a result of his church office. In 1982, the payroll of the Corporation of the President of the Church of Jesus Christ of Latter-day Saints (ie. the First

Presidency and their immediate aides) were estimated as <u>131.2 million!</u> A tidy sum for a church with no paid ministry."³¹ (Emphasis in the original)

Another contradiction can be found in the life of Joseph Smith himself. In his presumed First Vision **in 1820** he was forbidden twice to join a church.

> "...Joseph wrote that God told him that all Christian churches were wrong and all Christian beliefs 'were an abomination in his sight' (**Pearl of Great Price**, Joseph Smith—History 1:19). Thus, the beliefs of Christian people were declared to be offensive to God."³²

Yet,

> "...the young 'Prophet,' who by this time has had many angelic visits, has been led to the golden plates and is translating the Book of Mormon, proceeds **in 1828** to join the Methodist Church in Harmony, Pennsylvania. There is more than enough evidence to establish this as historical fact, and it is admitted even by Mormon writers. Joseph's wife, Emma, had been a Methodist since the age of seven, so Joseph may have joined the Methodists to please her—but join he did."³³

PARALLELS BETWEEN MORMONISM & MASONRY

There are so many contradictions in Mormonism, and as mentioned earlier, the teachings of the Mormon church today differ greatly from the teachings in the *Book of Mormon*. The following is a list of some of the Mormon doctrines that contradict the *Book of Mormon*.

> Celestial marriage for time and eternity
> Baptism for the dead
> God was once a man
> God has a body of flesh and bones
> Men can become Gods
> Polygamy

CHANGES IN MORMONISM

Mormonism has also changed throughout the years. Here are some of those changes:

"1. Changed from a monotheistic religion to a polytheistic religion.

2. Changed from an eternal God position to a non-eternal God position.

3. Changed from promoting Adam as their God to labeling this doctrine as false teaching and heresy.

4. Changed from an anti-Negro attitude to a pro-Negro attitude now allowing Blacks to partake of all the blessings of their church.

5. Changed from the teaching of monogamy to polygamy."[34]

The change from an anti-Negro attitude is very harmful to Mormon doctrine. You see, the Mormon Priesthood was forbidden to Negroes because the Mormon President, Brigham Young:

"...declared that one drop of Negro blood was sufficient to bring a person under the curse and bar him from the Priesthood...."

"He declared that if the time ever came when the Presidency and the Twelve Apostles should meet and CONFER THE PRIESTHOOD ON THE NEGROES, immediately THE PRIESTHOOD WOULD BE TAKEN FROM THE CHURCH AND THE CURSE BE GIVEN IN ITS PLACE. Prophet Young declared:

"'...the first presidency, the twelve, the high counsel, the Bishopric, and all elders of Israel, suppose we summon them to appear here, and here declare that it is right to mingle our seed, with the black race of Cain, that they shall come in with us and be partakers with us of all the blessings God has given to us. **On that very day, and from the hour we should do so, the priesthood is taken from this Church** and kingdom, and God leaves us to our fate. **The moment we consent to mingle with the seed of Cain, the Church must go to destruction,**—we should receive the curse which has been placed upon the seed of Cain, and never more be numbered with the children of Adam who are heirs to the Priesthood until that curse be removed.'"[35] (Capitals in the original; boldface added)

Another Mormon leader, Bruce McConkie, remarked: "As a result of his rebellion, Cain was cursed with a dark skin: he became the father of the Negroes, and those spirits who are not worthy to receive the priesthood, are born through his lineage."[36] Yet on June 1, 1978, the Presidency of the Mormon church voted to allow Negroes to hold the office of the Priesthood. By their own leaders' comments, this places the Mormon church under a curse and the "priesthood is taken from this Church and...the Church must go to destruction...."

The Bible tells us that in James 1:8 that "A double minded man is unstable in all his ways." The same is true of a church that keeps changing its doctrines. No wonder the Bible warns us: "BEWARE lest ye also, being led away with the error of the wicked, fall from your own stedfastness" (II Peter 3:17). "Therefore we ought to give the more earnest heed to the things which we have heard, lest at any time we should let them slip" (Hebrews 2:1).

Regardless of what man may say, the Bible is our final authority. No church can save you. Only Jesus Christ can do that. Even though you may be a moral and honest person, if you have never invited Christ into your heart as your own **PERSONAL** Savior, you, too, need to repent. Maybe you are not committing a blatant sin, but the Bible tells us that **"ALL** have sinned and come short of the glory of God" (Romans 3:23). The **"ALL"** includes both you and me, and "the wages of sin is [eternal] death; but the gift of God is eternal life through Jesus Christ our Lord" (Romans 6:23). God's gift to us is eternal life, but we must accept this gift to make the transaction valid. If I had a gift to give to you and you refused to accept it, that gift would do you no good. You must **RECEIVE** this gift for it to become effective.

SOME GOOD NEWS

Even though **ALL** of us are born in sin, the good news is that "Christ Jesus came into the world to save sinners" (I Timothy 1:15). If you have never accepted Christ as your **PERSONAL** Savior and would like to do so, the first step is to be born again. John 3:3 emphasizes: **"EXCEPT** a man be born **AGAIN,** he **CANNOT** see the kingdom of God." How can one be born **AGAIN?** We all know that we were born once, our physical birth, but can we enter into our mother's womb and be born the second time (see John 3:1-17)? No. The second birth comes by being born into the family of God. John 3:16: "For God so **LOVED** the world [that includes **YOU!**] that He **GAVE** His only Begotten Son, that **WHOSOEVER** [that includes **YOU**] **BELIEVETH** [trusts, clings to, relies on] Him [God's Son, Jesus] should not perish [in hell], but have everlasting life."

All you need to do is sincerely believe with all your heart that Jesus is the Son of God and to be willing to turn from your sins, whatever they are—big or small. Ask Jesus to come into your heart and help you to live for Him, and He **WILL** do it. "He that covereth his sins shall not prosper: but whoso **CONFESSETH AND FORSAKETH** them shall have mercy" (Proverbs 28:13). John 6:37 promises: "Him that cometh to Me I will **IN NO WISE** cast out." Romans 10:9 states: "If thou shalt **CONFESS** with thy mouth the Lord Jesus, and shalt **BELIEVE** in thine heart that God hath raised Him from the dead, thou **SHALT** be saved [born again]."

If you would like to be born again, pray your own prayer or sincerely pray the following: *Dear Jesus, I realize that I am a sinner. I believe that You died for my sins. Please forgive me of my past sins and come into my heart. Save me for Your sake, and help me to live for You. I ask this in Your name. Amen.*

If you sincerely prayed and asked Jesus to forgive you of your sins, you will have the assurance that you are now a child of God. John 1:12 reveals: "But **AS MANY AS RECEIVED HIM,** to them gave He power to become the sons of God, even to them that **BELIEVE** on His name." Read your Bible **EVERY** day (start with the book of John), and find a Bible-believing church where you can worship God with other born again believers.

"Therefore being justified by faith, we have peace with God through our Lord Jesus Christ" (Romans 5:1), "and the peace of God, which passeth all understanding, shall keep your hearts and minds through Christ Jesus" (Philippians 4:7). "If the Son [Jesus Christ] therefore shall make you free, ye shall be free indeed" (John 8:36).

ENDNOTES

CHAPTER 1: MORMONISM AND ITS HISTORY

[1] Bob Larson, *Larson's Book of Cults* (Wheaton, Illinois: Tyndale House Publishers, Inc., 1983), p. 157.

[2] *The Prophet Joseph Smith's Testimony* (Salt Lake City, Utah: The Church of Jesus Christ of Latter-day Saints), pp. 3, 4.

[3] Wesley P. Walters, *New Light on Mormon Origins from the Palmyra (N.Y.) Revival* (n.p., 1967), p. 19.

[4] *Ibid.*

[5] *Ibid.*, p. 5.

[6] Robert McKay, "Official First Vision Story False," *The Evangel* (October, 1991, Vol. 38, No. 7), p. 4.

[7] *The Prophet Joseph Smith's Testimony, op. cit.*, pp. 7-9.

[8] Walters, *op. cit.*, pp. 14-15.

[9] *The Prophet Joseph Smith's Testimony, op. cit.*, p. 9.

[10] *Ibid.* pp. 9-10.

[11] *Ibid.* pp. 11-12.

[12] *Ibid.* p. 17; LeGrand Richards, *A Marvelous Work and a Wonder* (Salt Lake City, Utah: Deseret Book Company, 1976), pp. 47-48; Fritz Ridenour, *So What's the Difference?* (Glendale, California: G/L Publications, 1967), pp. 154-157.

[13] *Testimony,* op. cit., pp. 18-19.

[14] See also *The Book of Mormon* (Alma 46:14-16) and *What of the Mormons?*, p. 1.

[15] Dave Hunt and Ed Decker, *The God Makers: A Shocking Expose of What the Mormon Church Really Believes* (Eugene, Oregon: Harvest House Publishers, 1984), pp. 245-246.

[16] Richards, *op. cit.*, p. 1.

[17] Gordon B. Hinckley, *What of the Mormons?* (Salt Lake City, Utah: The Church of Jesus Christ of Latter-day Saints, 1982), p. 11.

[18] *What the Mormons Think of Christ* (Salt Lake City, Utah: The Church of Jesus Christ of Latter-day Saints, 1982), p. 3.

[19] *What Is the Book of Mormon?* (Salt Lake City, Utah: The Church of Jesus Christ of Latter-day Saints, 1982), p. 1.

[20] Richards, *op. cit.,* p. 73.

[21] *The Book of Mormon* (Salt Lake City, Utah: The Church of Jesus Christ of Latter-day Saints, 1981); *Testimony, op. cit.,* p. 23.

[22] *Ibid.* p. 25.

[23] Richards, *op. cit.,* p. 54.

[24] Ridenour, *op. cit.,* p. 157.

[25] Rodger I. Anderson, *The Bible and Mormonism* (Grand Rapids, Michigan: Prayer and Tract League, n.d.), p. 9.

[26] *Plan of Salvation* (Salt Lake City, Utah: The Church of Jesus Christ of Latter-day Saints, 1978), p. 28.

[27] Richards, *op. cit.,* p. 55.

[28] "Scholars Probe Book of Mormon," *The News-Item* (June 26, 1993), p. 18.

[29] *Ibid.*

[30] "Mormonism Big, But a False Cult," *Calvary Contender* (September 15, 1997, Vol. 14, No. 18), p. 1.

[31] Robert A. McKay and John L. Smith, *Why Mormonism Is a Cult* (Marlow, Oklahoma, Utah Missions, Inc., 1985), p. 17.

[32] John L. Smith, *Who...Wrote the Book of Mormon???* (Marlow, Oklahoma: Utah Missions, Inc.), p. 3.

CHAPTER 2: SOME DOCTRINES OF MORMONISM

[1] See Mormon 9:9-10, 19; 10:34; 1 Nephi 11:32; 15:15; 2 Nephi 4:35; Helaman 12:8, etc.

[2] Robert A. McKay and John L. Smith, *Why Mormonism Is a Cult* (Marlow, Oklahoma: Utah Missions, Inc., 1985), p. 20.

[3] Walter Martin, *Walter Martin's Cults Reference Bible* (Santa Ana, California: Vision House, 1981), p. 47.

[4] McKay and Smith, *op. cit.*

[5] *Ibid.*

[6] *Ibid.*

[7] *Ibid.*

[8] *The Utah Evangel* (March 1987), p. 3.

[9] *Ibid.*

[10] *Journal of Discourses,* Vol. I, pp. 50-51.

[11] *Journal of Discourses,* Vol. VIII, p. 115.

[12] Ken R. Pulliam, "Why Mormonism Is Not Christianity," *Builder* (November/December 1992), p. 6.

[13] *What the Mormons Think of Christ* (Salt Lake City, Utah: The Church of Jesus Christ of Latter-day Saints, 1982), p. 22.

[14] *What of the Mormons?* (Salt Lake City, Utah: The Church of Jesus Christ of Latter-day Saints, 1982), p. 11.

[15] McKay and Smith, *op. cit.,* p. 22.

[16] Geoffrey Parrinder, ed., *World Religions: From Ancient History to the Present* (New York: The Hamlyn Publishing Group Limited, 1983), p. 99.

[17] Larry Davenport, *Mormonism...and the Bible: Does It Measure Up?* (La Mesa, California: Utah Christian Tract Society), p. 22.

[18] John Hornok, *Ten Reasons Why I Cannot Be a Mormon (Latter-Day Saint)* (Grandville, Michigan: Independent Fundamental Churches of America, 1976), p. 2.

[19] *The Utah Evangel* (July-August 1987), p. 7.

[20] *The Book of Mormon* (2 Nephi 25:23).

[21] LeGrand Richards, *A Marvelous Work and a Wonder* (Salt Lake City, Utah: Deseret Book Company, 1976), p. 24.

[22] Dave Hunt and Ed Decker, *The God Makers: A Shocking Expose of What the Mormon Church Really Believes* (Eugene, Oregon: Harvest House Publishers, 1984, p. 245.

[23] *What the Mormons Think of Christ, op. cit.,* p. 19.

[24] Bob Larson, *Larson's Book of Cults* (Wheaton, Illinois: Tyndale House Publishers, Inc., 1982), p. 161.

[25] *Journal of Discourses,* Vol. III, p. 247.

[26] McKay and Smith, *op. cit.*

[27] Fritz Ridenour, *So What's the Difference?* (Glendale, California: G/L Publications, 1967), p. 164.

[28] Rodger I. Anderson, *The Bible and Mormonism* (Grand Rapids, Michigan: Prayer and Tract League, n.d.), p. 18.

[29] *Doctrine and Covenants* (132:6, 19, 61-62).

[30] Sharon Lindbloom, "City of Joseph," *The Discerner* (July/August/September 1994, Vol. 14, No. 11), p. 9.

[31] Ridenour, *op. cit.,* p. 163.

[32] Lindbloom, *op. cit.*

[33] Hunt and Decker, quoting George Teasdale, *op. cit.,* p. 161.

[34] Hunt and Decker, quoting Orson Pratt, *Ibid.*

[35] *Ibid.,* p. 156.

[36] Hunt and Decker, quoting John J. Stewart, *Ibid.,* p. 169.

[37] Richards, *op. cit.,* p. 402.

[38] Hunt and Decker, quoting Wilford Woodruff, *op. cit.*

[39] Larson, *op. cit.*

[40] "Mormonism Big, But a False Cult," *Calvary Contender* (September 15, 1997, Vol. 14, No. 18), p. 1.

[41] McKay and Smith, *op. cit.*, p. 24.

[42] Robert McKay, "Portland Temple Facts," *The Evangel* (September 1989, Vol. 36, No. 6), p. 5.

[43] Richards, *op. cit.*, p. 306.

[44] Fritz Springmeier, *The Top 13 Illuminati Bloodlines* (Portland, Oregon: n.p., 1995), p. 223.

[45] *Ibid.*

[46] Hunt and Decker, *op. cit.*, pp. 187-188.

[47] Richards, *op. cit.*, pp. 188-189.

[48] Michael H. Reynolds, "Mormon Temples," *The Evangel* (July/August 1997, Vol. 44, No. 4), p. 13.

[49] "Massive Mormon Temple Plans Get Go-Ahead," *The News-Item* (December 14, 1996), p. 7.

[50] "Mormon Temples," *The Evangel, op. cit.*

[51] Rulon S. Howells, *The Mormon Story: A Pictorial Account of Mormonism* (Salt Lake City, Utah: Bookcraft, 1957), p. 80.

[52] Richards, *op. cit.*, p. 184. See also pp. 100, 106.

[53] "Mormon Temple Ritual" and "Mormon Temple Rituals Verbatim," Tapes from Chuck and Dolly Sackett.

[54] David Van Biema, "Kingdom Come," *Time* (August 4, 1997), pp. 55-56.

[55] C. E. Fleshman, "Cults a Curse to Christ and the Cross," *The Evangelist of Truth* (March 1986, Vol. 52, No. 3), p. 5.

[56] Robert McKay, "Who Is a False Prophet," *The Evangel* (October, 1991, Vol. 38, No. 7), p. 9.

[57] W. J. McK. McCormick, *Why Mormonism Is Not Christian* (n.p., n.d.), p. 6.

[58] McKay, "Who Is a False Prophet," *op. cit.*

[59] *Mormonism: The Christian View* (St. Louis, Missouri: Personal Freedom Outreach), p. 3.

CHAPTER 3: JOSEPH SMITH AND MAGIC

[1] "Satanic Rituals Reported Within Mormonism by Church Leader," *Saints Alive in Jesus* (November/December 1991), p. 2.

[2] Dave Hunt and Ed Decker, *The God Makers: A Shocking Expose of What the Mormon Church Really Believes* (Eugene, Oregon: Harvest House Publishers, 1984), p. 98.

[3] Jerald and Sandra Tanner, *Mormonism, Magic and Masonry* (n.p., n.d.), p. 19.

[4] *Ibid.*, p. 18.

[5] *Ibid.*

[6] "Satanic Rituals Reported Within Mormonism by Church Leader," *op. cit.*

[7] Tanner, *op. cit.*, p. 29.

[8] *Ibid.*

[9] Hunt and Decker, *op. cit.*, p. 94.

[10] Tanner, *op. cit.*, p. 1.

[11] *Ibid.*, p. 40.

[12] *Ibid.*

[13] Hunt and Decker, *op. cit.*, pp. 217-218.

[14] Tanner, *op. cit.*, p. 42.

[15] "Satanic Rituals Reported Within Mormonism by Church Leader," *op. cit.*

[16] Hunt and Decker, quoting Reed Durham, *op. cit.*, pp. 97-98.

[17] Fritz Ridenour, *So What's the Difference?* (Glendale, California: G/L Publications, 1967), p. 160.

[18] J. Edward Decker, *Birth of Heresy* (Saints Alive in Jesus, n.d.), p. 8. See also "A Letter to the Editor," *The Evangel* (October 1989; Vol. 36, No. 7), p. 4.

[19] Anton Szandor LaVey, *The Satanic Bible* (Avon Books, 1969), p. 145.

[20] Georgess McHargue, *Meet the Vampire* (1979), pp. 56-57.

[21] LaVey, *op. cit.*, p. 59.

[22] Edith Hamilton, *Mythology* (Boston, Massachusetts: Little, Brown and Company, 1942), p. 32; See also: Laurie Cabot with Tom Cowan, *Power of the Witch: The Earth, the Moon, and the Magical Path to Enlightenment* (New York, New York: Delacorte Press, 1989), p. 32; Percival George Woodcock, *Short Dictionary of Mythology* (Philosophical Library, 1953), p. 20; J. E. Cirlot (Translated by Jack Sage), *A Dictionary of Symbols* (New York: Dorset Press, 1991 Edition), pp. 81, 143; Harry E. Wedeck, *Treasury of Witchcraft* (New York, New York: Philosophical Library, 1961), pp. 39, 72.

[23] Laurie Cabot with Tom Cowan, *Power of the Witch: The Earth, the Moon, and the Magical Path to Enlightenment* (New York, New York: Delacorte Press, 1989), p. 32; See also: Harry E. Wedeck, *Treasury of Witchcraft* (New York, New York: Philosophical Library, 1961), pp. 39, 72; Eden Within (1994 Catalog), p. 12.

[24] Thomas Bulfinch, *Bulfinch's Mythology* (New York: Thomas Y. Crowell Company, Inc., 1970), p. 934; G. A. Riplinger, *New Age Bible Versions* (Munroe Falls, Ohio: A. V. Publications, 1993), p. 125; Frank Gaynor, Editor, *Dictionary of Mysticism* (New York: Philosophical Library, 1953), p. 76; Editors of Time-Life Books, *Magical Arts* (Alexandria, Virginia: Time-Life Books, 1990), p. 22.

[25] LeGrand Richards, *A Marvelous Work and a Wonder* (Salt Lake City, Utah: Deseret Book Company, 1976), p. 69.

[26] "Mormons Own Up to Joseph Smith's Occultism," *The Utah Evangel* (May-June 1987, Vol. 34, No. 4), p. 4.

CHAPTER 4: IS GODHOOD POSSIBLE?

[1] Gordon B. Hinckley, *What of the Mormons?* (Salt Lake City, Utah: The Church of Jesus Christ of Latter-day Saints, 1982), p. 8.

[2] *Doctrine and Covenants* 132:20.

[3] Robert A. McKay and John L. Smith, *Why Mormonism Is a Cult* (Marlow, Oklahoma: Utah Missions, Inc., 1985), p. 21.

[4] *Ibid.*

[5] Larry Davenport, *Mormonism...and the Bible: Does It Measure Up?* (La Mesa, California: Utah Christian Tract Society), p. 2.

[6] *Ibid.*, p. 6.

[7] LeGrand Richards, *A Marvelous Work and a Wonder* (Salt Lake City, Utah: Deseret Book Company, 1976), p. 303.

[8] Davenport, *op. cit.*, p. 12.

[9] Fritz Ridenour, *So What's the Difference?* (Glendale, California: G/L Publications, 1967), p. 163.

[10] Rodger I. Anderson, *The Bible and Mormonism* (Grand Rapids, Michigan: Prayer and Tract League, n.d.), pp. 14-15.

[11] Note: The endowment ceremony was greatly changed as of April 1990. The temple ritual deleted the blood oaths, the mocking of Christian pastors, the Pay lay ale chant, and the Masonic five points of fellowship. Also deleted were several items that many LDS women found repugnant.

[12] Dave Hunt and Ed Decker, quoting George Teasdale in *The God Makers: A Shocking Expose of What the Mormon Church Really Believes* (Eugene, Oregon: Harvest House Publishers, 1984), p. 190.

[13] For more information on the temple ceremonies listen to the tapes on Mormonism by former Mormons Chuck and Dolly Sackett.

[14] Ed Decker, *Temple of the God Makers* (Issaquah, Washington: Saints Alive in Jesus, 1985), p. 11.

[15] *Ibid.*

110 MORMONISM, MASONRY, AND GODHOOD

[16] In an article in the September 1990 issue of *The Evangel* entitled "MORMON TEMPLE RITUALS DRASTICALLY RENOVATED IN SECRET" by Chuck and Dolly Sackett, we find: "The Masonically inspired **Five Points of Fellowship** through the **temple veil** has been eliminated. No longer will temple initiates be required to embrace 'the Lord' through the veil in this mystical, highly occultic configuration while they whisper in his ear the **Name of the Second Token of the Melchizedec Priesthood, the Patriarchal Grip, or Sure Sign of the Nail.** The embrace is **out** but it is likely that the **incantation** associated with it is still **in.**" (Emphasis in the original)

[17] Stewart Farrar, *What Witches Do: The Modern Coven Revealed* (Custer, Washington: Phoenix Publishing Company, 1983), p. 15.

[18] William and Sharon Schnoebelen, *Lucifer Dethroned* (Chino, California: Chick Publications, 1993), p. 241.

[19] *Ibid.*

[20] Alex Horne, *King Solomon's Temple in the Masonic Tradition* (London, England: The Aquarian Press, 1971), p. 345.

[21] Tract written by Jim Shaw entitled *Mormonism and Freemasonry.*

[22] Dave Hunt, *The Cult Explosion* (Eugene, Oregon: Harvest House Publishers, 1980), p. 77.

[23] Frederic Schumann, *Mormonism* (St. Louis, Missouri: Concordia Tract Mission, 1983), p. 14.

[24] W. L. Wilmshurst, *The Meaning of Masonry* (Bell Publishing Company, reprint of fifth edition published in 1927), p. 31.

[25] For more information on Masonry, see *Hidden Secrets of Masonry.* This book can be purchased for $4.95 plus $1.05 postage from Sharing, 212 E. 7th Street (O), Mt. Carmel, Pennsylvania 17851-2211.

[26] Richards, *op. cit.,* p. 191.

[26] *Ibid.* p. 300.

CHAPTER 5: PARALLELS BETWEEN MORMONISM AND MASONRY

[1] W. J. McK. McCormick, *Christ, the Christian, and Freemasonry* (Belfast, Ireland: Great Joy Publications, 1984), pp. 97-98.

ENDNOTES

[2] For more information on the New Age Movement, see *Questions and Answers About the New Age Movement,* which is available through Sharing.

[3] *The Mormon Cult* (Liberty, South Carolina: Highway and Hedges Tracts), pp. 9-10.

[4] Dave Hunt and Ed Decker, *The God Makers: A Shocking Expose of What the Mormon Church Really Believes* (Eugene, Oregon: Harvest House Publishers, 1984), p. 255.

[5] *Ibid.*

[6] *Ibid.*

[7] David Van Biema, "Kingdom Come," *Time* (August 4, 1997), p. 52.

[8] *Ibid.*

[9] *The Mormon Cult, op. cit.,* pp. 10-11.

[10] *The Perilous Times* (September 1994, Vol. 16, No. 7), p. 3.

[11] *The Mormon Cult, op. cit.,* p. 12.

[12] *Ibid.*

[13] *Utah Evangel* (March 1987), p. 1.

[14] *The Perilous Times, op. cit.*

[15] *Time, op. cit.,* pp. 53-54.

[16] *Ibid.,* p. 54.

[17] "Parents Barred from Wedding Are Angry at Mormon Church" (Newspaper article dated July 15, 1990), p. 1B.

[18] *Ibid.,* p. 3B.

[19] *Ibid.,* p. 1B.

[20] *Saints Alive in Jesus Newsletter* (April 1992), p. 3.

[21] *Ibid.*

[22] Lloyd C. Button, *No Longer a Mormon* (Minneapolis, Minnesota: Religious Analysis Service, Inc.), pp. 3-4.

[23] Mike Carter, "Mormons Move to Defeat Effort to Legalize Horse-Race Gambling," *The Arizona Daily Star* (May 31, 1992, Section B), p. 9.

[24] Robert McKay, "Suicide in Utah," *The Evangel* (October, 1991, Vol. 38, No. 7), p. 6.

[25] "Utah Suicides," *The Evangel* (July/August 1997, Vol. 44, No. 4), p. 7.

[26] *"...And Ye Shall Be As God"* (St. Louis, Missouri: Personal Freedom Outreach), p. 3.

[27] John L. Smith, "Sex Abuse Article," *The Evangel* (October, 1991, Vol. 38, No. 7), p. 3.

[28] Hilary Groutage, "Support Group for Divorced Women Seeks Niche Within Mormon Church," *The Arizona Daily Star* (December 1, 1991, Section B), p. 9.

[29] William J. Schnoebelen, *The Seventeen "Straw Men" of the True Church* (Issaquah, Washington: Saints Alive in Jesus, 1987), p. 1.

[30] *Ibid.*, p. 3.

[31] *Ibid.*, pp. 6-7.

[32] Robert McKay, "Mormonism's Confusion," *The Utah Evangel* (May-June 1987, Vol. 34, No. 4), p. 6.

[33] Hunt and Decker, *op. cit.*, pp. 216-217.

[34] *Mormonism: The Christian View* (St. Louis, Missouri: Personal Freedom Outreach), p. 3.

[35] *Oops There Goes the Priesthood* (La Mesa, California: Utah Christian Tract Society), pp. 2-3.

[36] *Ibid.*, p. 3.

BIBLIOGRAPHY

(The following is a partial listing of the reference materials that were used in preparing this book.)

"*...And Ye Shall Be As God*" (St. Louis, Missouri: Personal Freedom Outreach).

Anderson, Rodger I. *The Bible and Mormonism* (Grand Rapids, Michigan: Prayer and Tract League, n.d.).

Book of Mormon, The (Salt Lake City, Utah: The Church of Jesus Christ of Latter-day Saints, 1981).

Bulfinch, Thomas. *Bulfinch's Mythology* (New York: Thomas Y. Crowell Company, Inc., 1970).

Button, Lloyd C. *No Longer a Mormon* (Minneapolis, Minnesota: Religious Analysis Service, Inc.).

Cabot, Laurie with Cowan, Tom. *Power of the Witch: The Earth, the Moon, and the Magical Path to Enlightenment* (New York, New York: Delacorte Press, 1989).

Carter, Mike. "Mormons Move to Defeat Effort to Legalize Horse-Race Gambling," *The Arizona Daily Star* (May 31, 1992, Section B).

Cirlot, J. E. (Translated by Jack Sage), *A Dictionary of Symbols* (New York: Dorset Press, 1991 Edition).

Davenport, Larry. *Mormonism...and the Bible: Does It Measure Up?* (La Mesa, California: Utah Christian Tract Society).

Decker, Ed. *Temple of the God Makers* (Issaquah, Washington: Saints Alive in Jesus, 1985).

Decker, J. Edward. *Birth of Heresy* (Saints Alive in Jesus, n.d.), p. 8. See also "A Letter to the Editor," *The Evangel* (October 1989; Vol. 36, No. 7).

Doctrine and Covenants.

Eden Within (1994 Catalog).

Editors of Time-Life Books, *Magical Arts* (Alexandria, Virginia: Time-Life Books, 1990).

Farrar, Stewart. *What Witches Do: The Modern Coven Revealed* (Custer, Washington: Phoenix Publishing Company, 1983).

Fleshman, C. E. "Cults a Curse to Christ and the Cross," *The Evangelist of Truth* (March 1986, Vol. 52, No. 3).

Gaynor, Frank, Editor. *Dictionary of Mysticism* (New York: Philosophical Library, 1953).

Groutage, Hilary. "Support Group for Divorced Women Seeks Niche Within Mormon Church," *The Arizona Daily Star* (December 1, 1991, Section B).

Hamilton, Edith. *Mythology* (Boston, Massachusetts: Little, Brown and Company, 1942).

Hinckley, Gordon B. *What of the Mormons?* (Salt Lake City, Utah: The Church of Jesus Christ of Latter-day Saints, 1982).

Horne, Alex. *King Solomon's Temple in the Masonic Tradition* (London, England: The Aquarian Press, 1971).

Hornok, John. *Ten Reasons Why I Cannot Be a Mormon (Latter-Day Saint)* (Grandville, Michigan: Independent Fundamental Churches of America, 1976).

Howells, Rulon S. *The Mormon Story: A Pictorial Account of Mormonism* (Salt Lake City, Utah: Bookcraft, 1957).

Hunt, Dave. *The Cult Explosion* (Eugene, Oregon: Harvest House Publishers, 1980).

Hunt, Dave and Decker, Ed. *The God Makers: A Shocking Expose of What the Mormon Church Really Believes* (Eugene, Oregon: Harvest House Publishers, 1984).

Larson, Bob. *Larson's Book of Cults* (Wheaton, Illinois: Tyndale House Publishers, Inc., 1983).

LaVey, Anton Szandor. *The Satanic Bible* (Avon Books, 1969).

Lindbloom, Sharon. "City of Joseph," *The Discerner* (July/August/September 1994, Vol. 14, No. 11).

BIBLIOGRAPHY 115

Martin, Walter. *Walter Martin's Cults Reference Bible* (Santa Ana, California: Vision House, 1981).

"Massive Mormon Temple Plans Get Go-Ahead," *The News-Item* (December 14, 1996).

McCormick, W. J. McK. *Christ, the Christian, and Freemasonry* (Belfast, Ireland: Great Joy Publications, 1984).

McCormick, W. J. McK. *Why Mormonism Is Not Christian* (n.p., n.d.).

McHargue, Georgess. *Meet the Vampire* (1979).

McKay, Robert. "Mormonism's Confusion," *The Utah Evangel* (May-June 1987, Vol. 34, No. 4).

McKay, Robert. "Official First Vision Story False," *The Evangel* (October, 1991, Vol. 38, No. 7).

McKay, Robert. "Suicide in Utah," *The Evangel* (October, 1991, Vol. 38, No. 7).

McKay, Robert. "Who Is a False Prophet," *The Evangel* (October, 1991, Vol. 38, No. 7).

McKay, Robert A. and Smith, John L. *Why Mormonism Is a Cult* (Marlow, Oklahoma, Utah Missions, Inc., 1985).

Mormon Cult, The (Liberty, South Carolina: Highway and Hedges Tracts).

Mormonism: The Christian View (St. Louis, Missouri: Personal Freedom Outreach).

"Mormonism Big, But a False Cult," *Calvary Contender* (September 15, 1997, Vol. 14, No. 18).

"Mormons Own Up to Joseph Smith's Occultism," *The Utah Evangel* (May-June 1987, Vol. 34, No. 4).

Oops There Goes the Priesthood (La Mesa, California: Utah Christian Tract Society).

"Parents Barred from Wedding Are Angry at Mormon Church" (Newspaper article dated July 15, 1990).

Parrinder, Geoffrey, Editor. *World Religions: From Ancient History to the Present* (New York: The Hamlyn Publishing Group Limited, 1983).

Perilous Times, The (September 1994, Vol. 16, No. 7).

Plan of Salvation (Salt Lake City, Utah: The Church of Jesus Christ of Latter-day Saints, 1978).

Prophet Joseph Smith's Testimony, The (Salt Lake City, Utah: The Church of Jesus Christ of Latter-day Saints).

Pulliam, Ken R. "Why Mormonism Is Not Christianity," *Builder* (November/December 1992).

Michael H. Reynolds, "Mormon Temples," *The Evangel* (July/August 1997, Vol. 44, No. 4).

Richards, LeGrand. *A Marvelous Work and a Wonder* (Salt Lake City, Utah: Deseret Book Company, 1976).

Ridenour, Fritz. *So What's the Difference?* (Glendale, California: G/L Publications, 1967).

Riplinger, G. A. *New Age Bible Versions* (Munroe Falls, Ohio: A. V. Publications, 1993).

Saints Alive in Jesus Newsletter (April 1992).

"Satanic Rituals Reported Within Mormonism by Church Leader," *Saints Alive in Jesus* (November/December 1991).

Schnoebelen, William and Sharon. *Lucifer Dethroned* (Chino, California: Chick Publications, 1993).

Schnoebelen, William J. *The Seventeen "Straw Men" of the True Church* (Issaquah, Washington: Saints Alive in Jesus, 1987).

"Scholars Probe Book of Mormon," *The News-Item* (June 26, 1993).

Schumann, Frederic. *Mormonism* (St. Louis, Missouri: Concordia Tract Mission, 1983).

Shaw, Jim. Tract entitled *Mormonism and Freemasonry*.

Smith, John L. "Sex Abuse Article," *The Evangel* (October, 1991, Vol. 38, No. 7).

Smith, John L. *Who...Wrote the Book of Mormon???* (Marlow, Oklahoma: Utah Missions, Inc.).

Springmeier, Fritz. *The Top 13 Illuminati Bloodlines* (Portland, Oregon: n.p., 1995).

Tanner, Jerald and Sandra. *Mormonism, Magic and Masonry* (n.p., n.d.).

Utah Evangel, The (July-August 1987).

Utah Evangel, The (March 1987).

Van Biema, David. "Kingdom Come," *Time* (August 4, 1997).

Walters, Wesley P. *New Light on Mormon Origins from the Palmyra (N.Y.) Revival* (n.p., 1967).

Wedeck, Harry E. *Treasury of Witchcraft* (New York, New York: Philosophical Library, 1961).

What Is the Book of Mormon? (Salt Lake City, Utah: The Church of Jesus Christ of Latter-day Saints, 1982).

What of the Mormons? (Salt Lake City, Utah: The Church of Jesus Christ of Latter-day Saints, 1982).

What the Mormons Think of Christ (Salt Lake City, Utah: The Church of Jesus Christ of Latter-day Saints, 1982).

Wilmshurst, W. L. *The Meaning of Masonry* (Bell Publishing Company, reprint of fifth edition published in 1927).

Woodcock, Percival George. *Short Dictionary of Mythology* (Philosophical Library, 1953).

Index

Aaronic Priesthood......................................12, 76, 80, 82
Abaddon..24
Abrac..54
Abracadabra...54
Adam....................34, 35, 47, 68, 69, 71, 72, 81, 84, 97, 99
Adam and Eve...67, 68, 69, 71, 72, 78
Advocate..88
AgReserves, Inc..89
Ahab..27, 28
alcoholic..89, 91, 94
all-seeing eye..75
angel......6, 7, 10, 15, 16, 17, 19, 20, 21, 22, 23, 24, 25, 26, 27,
....................................28, 29, 30, 31, 45, 56, 58, 67, 86, 88, 96
angel of light..25
Anthon, Charles..10, 11
anti-Negro...97
Apollyon...24
apron...71, 75, 78, 83
archaeological...14, 18, 19
Arizona Daily Star..92
Arizona Republic...87
Article of Faith..51
Articles of Faith..17
ascension...15
astrologer..61
astrological seals..46
astrology..61
AT&T...88
athame..46
atonement..40

baptism............................11, 15, 19, 31, 32, 50, 51, 65, 90, 97
baptized on behalf of the dead..50
beehive..75
Beneficial Life Insurance...88, 89
Bennett, John C. 75
blasphemy...36
blood..70
Blood Atonement..39
blood oaths..76, 77
Bonneville International...89
Book of Mormon...8, 11, 13, 14, 15, 16, 17, 18, 19, 32, 36, 40,
....59, 63, 64, 68, 96, 97
Borden Products...88
born again..100
Boy Scout..94
Brewster, James Colin..45
Brigham Young University..37, 85
Brite Music..89

Brockbank, Bernard..36
Buddha..86
Button, Lloyd C. 92
BYU..37

Cabot, Laurie..64
caduceus...57
CARP..85
Catholic Church...89
CAUSA..85, 86
ceremonies for the dead..49
channel...28
charmer..65
Cheesman, Paul R. 6
Child abuse..94
Christ.....6, 12, 13, 20, 21, 22, 24, 26, 27, 30, 32, 35, 36, 37,
.........................38, 39, 40, 42, 49, 79, 80, 86, 95, 99, 100, 101
Christian Right..86
Christ's blood cannot atone for certain sins...........................39
Chrysler..88
Church of Christ..95
Church of Jesus Christ of Latter-day Saints............6, 12, 13, 49, 95
Church of the Latter-day Saints...95
CIA..87
clasped hands..76
Clinton, Hillary..20
communion..15
Communism..86
compass...69, 75, 84
Congress...87
conjure..56
contradictions..97
contradictory instructions..67
counterfeit..16
Cowdery, Oliver...11, 12, 15, 16
crime...93
Crowley, Aleister...74
crucifixion..15, 40
crystal-ball gazing...55
Cumorah..8, 15, 56

Dallas Times Herald..88
dances...92
Daniel..29
Decker, Ed...46, 70, 73, 75
deliverance...30
demon...56
Denver Post..88
Dern, George..93
Deseret Book Co..90
Deseret Cattle & Citrus Ranch...89

Deseret Farms of California..........88
Deseret Farms of Texas..........88
Deseret Livestock Ranch..........88
Deseret News..........90, 93
Deseret Ranch of Canada..........88
Deseret Ranch of Florida..........88
Devil..........12, 13, 24, 27, 31
DeZeng, Philip M...........57
divination..........54, 65
divining..........5, 56
divining rod..........54, 57
divorce..........92, 93
Doctrine and Covenants..........13, 16, 33, 37, 40, 52, 66
dowsing..........57
drinking..........92
drug use..........91
druidic priests..........73
drunkenness..........92
DuPont..........88
Durham, Reed..........60

Eagle Marketing..........89
ecumenism..........86
Elberta Farms..........88
enchant..........25, 26, 59, 65
endowment ceremony..........69, 71
endowments..........78
erroneous teaching..........38
esoteric..........60
eternal progression..........19, 49
Evangel..........94
evil spirit..........24, 25, 26

F.B.I...........85, 87
fallen angel..........20, 24
false Christ..........27
false doctrine..........24, 38
false prophet..........25, 26, 27, 52, 53
familiar spirit..........64
family-oriented..........90, 91
Farrell's Ice Cream Parlours..........89
FBI..........87
Feathered Serpent..........37
fertility..........37
Five Points of Fellowship..........72, 74, 75, 76, 83
Fivefold Kiss..........74
Flaming Torch..........89
Ford..........88
fornication..........40
fortune telling..........5
fraud..........7, 93

Entry	Pages
Freeman Foundation	85
Freeman Institute	85, 86, 87
gambling	92
Garden of Eden	34, 47, 67
gavel	84
gay bars	94
genealogical record	51
General Motors	88
General Relief Society	94
ghost	55, 59, 63
glass-looking	55, 57
God and Freedom Banquet	85
god of death	37
God was once a man	32, 33, 97
godhood	33, 36, 44, 51, 66, 67, 71, 78
gods	19, 26, 33, 44, 52, 53, 66, 67, 84
gold plates	7, 8, 9, 10, 18, 56, 59, 96
Goodwin, S. H.	77
Grand Pontiff	78
Grant, Brigham S.	93
Grant, Heber J.	93
Grant, Jedeliah	40
Great Rite	74
Greenwich Times	88
guardian angel	20
Gucumatz	37
Hancock, Muriel	90
Hancock, Norman	90, 91
handfasting	45
Harris, Martin	10, 11, 15, 16, 59
Hartford Currant	88
Hecate	64
hell	12, 13, 24, 32, 67, 100
Herod	21
Hicks, Eldon	69
Hiram Abiff	60
hobgoblin	55
holdings of the Mormon church	87
Holy Ghost	12, 21, 32, 35, 36, 50
homosexual	94
Horne, Alex	74
horse race	93
Hot Shoppes	89
Hotel Temple Square Co	90
Hyustus	37
IBM	88
Ideal Corporation	89
Illa-Tici	37

incantation..46, 73
Indian...14, 18
Intermountain Sexual Abuse Treatment Center..............94

J.C. Penney..88
Jack, Elaine..94
Jacobs, Henry B. 41
Jacobs, Zina D. Huntington...41
Jesus...5, 6, 12, 13, 15, 20, 21, 22, 30, 32, 35, 36, 37, 40, 42,
....49, 74, 86, 95, 99, 100, 101
Jesus was not virgin-born..36
Jesus was the spirit brother of Lucifer........................37
Journal of Discourses..36, 40
Jupiter..60, 61
Jupiter talisman...60

Kana..37
Kanaloa..37
Kane...37
killing...63
Kimball, Heber C. 75
King Ranch..89
KMEO-AM-FM...87
Knight Kadosh...83
Knights of Malta..83
Knights of the Sun...84
Kodak...88
Kolob..34, 86
Kon...37

lamia..63
Lapham, Fayette..54, 58
Latter-day Saints..35, 42, 89
LDS...19, 44, 45, 88, 90, 93, 94
LDS Institute of Religion..60
LDS Welfare Farms & Diaries....................................88
Lee, John D. 41
Lewis, Heil...59
light...5, 7, 12, 24, 25, 113, 117
liquor..92
Lono...37
Lucifer...24, 31, 37, 71, 72, 73, 81
lying spirit..28
lying wonder..27

Macumba..70
magic.....5, 10, 17, 25, 26, 45, 46, 53, 54, 56, 57, 60, 61, 64,
....65, 70
magic circles..54
magic rods...56
magic seals..61

magic underwear..46
magick staff...46
marriage........19, 42, 43, 44, 45, 46, 47, 50, 67, 78, 90, 91, 97
Marriott Hotel...89, 91
martyr..63
Mason..................................32, 72, 74, 75, 78, 79, 81, 83, 84
Masonic...60, 69, 71, 75, 78, 83, 94
Masonry......................59, 71, 72, 74, 75, 78, 81, 82, 83, 84
McConkie, Bruce...6, 33, 37, 99
McCormick, W.J. McK..82
McKay, David O. 85
McKay, Robert...6, 19, 44
Meadow Fresh Farms..88
Melchisedec..80
Melchizedek....................................12, 32, 70, 76, 78, 79
men can become gods...67, 97
men on the moon..52
Methodist Church...96
Michael..35, 71
miracle...25, 26, 27, 32
money digging..54
Mormo..63, 64
Mormon...5, 6, 10, 11, 12, 13, 14, 15, 16, 17, 18, 19, 31, 32, 33, 35,
36, 37, 38, 39, 40, 41, 42, 43, 44, 45, 46, 49, 50, 51, 52, 53, 54, 60,
62, 63, 64, 65, 66, 67, 68, 69, 70, 71, 72, 73, 74, 75, 76, 77, 78, 79,
80, 81, 82, 83, 84, 85, 86, 87, 88, 89, 90, 91, 92, 93, 94, 95,
....96, 97, 99
Mormon History Association..60
Mormon wealth...89
Moroni..6, 7, 8, 9, 10, 15, 17, 19, 31, 56, 59
Moses...25, 26, 68, 80, 86
Myung, Sun Moon..85, 86, 87

Nabisco...88
National Center for Constitutional Studies.........................85
Nauvoo Expositor..62
necromancer...65
necromancy..54, 56
Neely, Albert..57
Negro...97, 98, 99
New Age..84, 85, 87, 94
New Agers..72
New Era..84
new name..47, 70, 76, 84
Newsday..88
nudity..46

oath...83
oaths...32, 70, 77
observer of times..65
occult...5, 28, 54, 56, 57, 59, 60, 62, 63, 65, 73, 74, 94, 115

Orange Coast Daily Pilot 88
ouija board 20

paid ministry 95
palmistry 65
Pay lay ale 72
Pearl of Great Price 6, 13, 68, 96
penalty 76, 82
perfection 49
Peter 12, 29, 30, 99
Petersen, Mark E. 37
plates 9, 10, 11, 15, 16, 59
Plumed Serpent 37
Poffarl, Fred 57
polygamy 31, 32, 40, 41, 42, 43, 44, 62, 97
Polynesian Cultural Center 90
polytheistic 97
pornographic movies 89, 91
Pratt, Orson 33, 36, 40, 42
premortal existence 36
priesthood 12, 15, 42, 46, 47, 50, 70, 71, 72, 73, 74, 76, 78,
.... 79, 80, 82, 97, 98, 99
prophet 6, 8, 14, 26, 27, 28, 41, 42, 43, 44, 51, 52, 53, 56,
.... 60, 64, 85, 86, 96, 98
protection 29, 30, 47
proxy 45

Queen of the Witches 64
Quetzalcoatl 37

racing 93
reincarnation 38
Representatives 87
resurrection 70
revelation 17, 32, 41, 42, 43, 44, 50, 56, 85
revival 5, 6
Richards, LeGrand 13, 16, 17, 38, 45, 47, 50, 64, 67, 78
Robey, Carlos Y. 94
Rod of Aaron 57
Roman Catholic 89
Roy Rogers 89
Royal Arch 84

sacrifice 56
Salt Lake Tribune 91, 93, 94
salvation 38, 39, 42, 43, 44, 49, 50
Santeria 70
Satan 9, 13, 22, 24, 25, 27, 45, 46, 63, 65, 70, 71, 72, 74, 81, 84
Satan worship 73
Satanic Bible 63
Schnoebelen, Bill 95

Scott, Walter..45
scrying...55
seal..45
seal of Mars..46
sealed..48, 70
sealed marriage..31, 32
sealing..45
sealing ceremonies...46, 90
sealing of marriages..45
secrecy...82
seducing doctrine..31
seducing spirit....................................24, 25, 27, 31
seer stones...45
Senators...87
serpent...46
sexual abuse..94
sexual intercourse...74
Shell Oil..88
Shibboleth...82
Sign of the Nail...83
signs and wonders...27
Skousen, Cleon...85, 86
Smith, Hyrum..75
Smith, Joseph....5, 6, 7, 8, 9, 10, 11, 12, 15, 16, 17, 18, 19, 26, 31, 33, 38, 41, 42, 45, 46, 47, 52, 53, 54, 55, 56, 57, 59, 60, 61, 63, 64, 65, ...66, 70, 75, 78, 86, 87, 90, 96
Snow, Lorenzo..33
sorcery...64
speaking in tongues...32
spectacles..11
spirit beings..69
spirit children..32
spirit world..65
spirits.................20, 23, 24, 25, 26, 27, 50, 58, 64, 65, 69, 99
Sporting News..88
square...69, 76, 84
square and compasses...84
Stafford, Joshua...55
Stafford, William..56
Stewart, John J..43
Stewart, Ora Pate..67
suicide..93
Sume..37
superstition..75
swapping wives...41

talisman..60, 61, 62, 70
Talmage, James...66
Taylor, John...12
Teasdale, George...42
teen pregnancies..93

Temple marriage..44
temple recommend..90, 91
temple work is done on behalf of the dead.....................50
Templeview Farms..89
theft..16
Time...19, 20, 51, 87, 89
Times..88
Times-Mirror...88
tithing..51
tobacco..91
Tongo-roa...37
treasure hunt..5
Tubal Cain...83

U&I, Inc. 88
undergarment...69, 71, 84
underworld..37, 64
Unification Church..85, 86, 87
Union Carbide..88
Union Pacific..88
universal salvation...32, 49
University of Utah...60
Urim and Thummim...9, 10
Utah Historical Quarterly...92

vagrancy..7
vampires..63
vengeance...83
vicariously married..47
Viracocha..37
vision...5, 6, 7, 54, 96, 115
voodoo...70
Votan...37

Walters, Wesley P. 57
warlocks..73
Whitmer, David..16
Wilmshurst, W.L. 78
witch..64, 65, 74
witchcraft......................................45, 54, 56, 64, 65, 73, 74, 75
Wixepechocha..37
wizard..65
Woodruff, Wilford..43, 44
world ruler..86

ye shall be as gods..84
Young, Brigham...12, 33, 34, 35, 38, 39, 40, 41, 66, 75, 97, 98
Yurika Foods..85

ZCMI 89

NOTES:

NOTES:

NOTES:

NOTES:

ORDER BLANK

BOOKS:
- ____ *A New World Order Is Coming* (116 pages)...............$ 5.95
- ____ *A Scriptural View of Hell* (40 pages).......................$ 4.95
- ____ *Alcoholics Anonymous Unmasked* (320 pages)...........$11.95
- ____ *Billy Graham and His Friends* (800 pages)................$21.95
- ____ *Hidden Secrets of Masonry* (64 pages).......................$ 4.95
- ____ *Hidden Secrets of the Eastern Star* (512 pages)...........$15.95
- ____ *Masonic and Occult Symbols Illustrated* (552 pages)..$21.95
- ____ *Mormonism, Masonry, and Godhood* (132 pages).......$ 6.95
- ____ *Pathway to Peace* (72 pages)....................................$2.50
- ____ *Secure in Christ* (136 pages)......................................$ 6.95
- ____ *Tongues, Prosperity, and Godhood* (192 pages)............$8.95

BOOKLETS: ....$ .50 each
- ____ Astrology and Your Future
- ____ Different Types of Friendship
- ____ Dowsing Is in the Bible!
- ____ Eastern Star Goddesses
- ____ Explanation of Some Occult Terms
- ____ Hidden Dangers of Reflexology
- ____ Hypnosis: Cure or Curse?
- ____ Questions and Answers About the New Age Movement
- ____ To Catholics with Love
- ____ What Is Your I.Q.?

ARTICLES: ....$ .50 each
- ____ Chart Your Course with Orion International
- ____ Divination
- ____ I Have Sinned
- ____ Jason Winters and His Herbal Tea
- ____ March for Jesus (WHICH Jesus?)

____ New Age Love
____ Should We Name Names?
____ The Rapture—When Will It Occur?
____ Unity or D-i-v-i-s-i-o-n?
____ What Is Miscegenation?
____ Witchcraft in the Church
____ Ye Shall Not Surely Die

MORE ARTICLES:

____ Jay Gary: The Millennium Doctor...............................$4.00
____ Little Known Facts About Focus on the Family.............$4.00
____ Masons Pay Tribute to Billy Graham..........................$1.00
____ Unholy Laughter? (2 part series)...............................$1.00

TRACTS: ....$ .05 each

____ A Perfect Church (Malcolm Burns)
____ ABC's of Salvation
____ Divorce and Remarriage
____ I've Been Cheated! (Jean Burns)
____ My God Cannot Do Everything
____ Treasure of All Ages (Jean Burns)
____ What Are You Missing? (Jean Burns)
____ What Is Sin?

____ **SUBTOTAL**
____ **POSTAGE** (10% of order [$1.00 mininum; $6.00 maximum])
____ **DONATION FOR BIBLES & LITERATURE FOR JAIL**
____ **TOTAL ENCLOSED**

For orders, or a complete list of literature available, write to:
SHARING
212 East Seventh Street (O2)
Mt. Carmel, PA 17851-2211

ORDER BLANK

BOOKS:
- ____ *A New World Order Is Coming* (116 pages)...............$ 5.95
- ____ *A Scriptural View of Hell* (40 pages).......................$ 4.95
- ____ *Alcoholics Anonymous Unmasked* (320 pages)...........$11.95
- ____ *Billy Graham and His Friends* (800 pages)................$21.95
- ____ *Hidden Secrets of Masonry* (64 pages).....................$ 4.95
- ____ *Hidden Secrets of the Eastern Star* (512 pages)...........$15.95
- ____ *Masonic and Occult Symbols Illustrated* (552 pages)..$21.95
- ____ *Mormonism, Masonry, and Godhood* (132 pages).......$ 6.95
- ____ *Pathway to Peace* (72 pages)..................................$2.50
- ____ *Secure in Christ* (136 pages).................................$ 6.95
- ____ *Tongues, Prosperity, and Godhood* (192 pages)............$8.95

BOOKLETS: ....$ .50 each
- ____ Astrology and Your Future
- ____ Different Types of Friendship
- ____ Dowsing Is in the Bible!
- ____ Eastern Star Goddesses
- ____ Explanation of Some Occult Terms
- ____ Hidden Dangers of Reflexology
- ____ Hypnosis: Cure or Curse?
- ____ Questions and Answers About the New Age Movement
- ____ To Catholics with Love
- ____ What Is Your I.Q.?

ARTICLES: ....$ .50 each
- ____ Chart Your Course with Orion International
- ____ Divination
- ____ I Have Sinned
- ____ Jason Winters and His Herbal Tea
- ____ March for Jesus (WHICH Jesus?)

____ New Age Love
____ Should We Name Names?
____ The Rapture—When Will It Occur?
____ Unity or D-i-v-i-s-i-o-n?
____ What Is Miscegenation?
____ Witchcraft in the Church
____ Ye Shall Not Surely Die

MORE ARTICLES:
____ Jay Gary: The Millennium Doctor..............................$4.00
____ Little Known Facts About Focus on the Family.............$4.00
____ Masons Pay Tribute to Billy Graham..........................$1.00
____ Unholy Laughter? (2 part series)................................$1.00

TRACTS: ....$ .05 each
____ A Perfect Church (Malcolm Burns)
____ ABC's of Salvation
____ Divorce and Remarriage
____ I've Been Cheated! (Jean Burns)
____ My God Cannot Do Everything
____ Treasure of All Ages (Jean Burns)
____ What Are You Missing? (Jean Burns)
____ What Is Sin?

_____ **SUBTOTAL**
_____ **POSTAGE** (10% of order [$1.00 mininum; $6.00 maximum])
_____ **DONATION FOR BIBLES & LITERATURE FOR JAIL**
_____ **TOTAL ENCLOSED**

For orders, or a complete list of literature available, write to:
SHARING
212 East Seventh Street (O2)
Mt. Carmel, PA 17851-2211

A NEW WORLD ORDER IS COMING

"Peace, peace, we must have peace at any cost," is the cry being heard from every quarter today. If we don't soon agree to have a peaceful world, we may all die in a nuclear holocaust. So, what will it take to have a peaceful co-existence? The answer given is the establishment of a one world government. In addition to a one world government, there will be a one world religion and a one world economy. What is also needed in a one world government is a leader. Who will this leader be?

In spite of many plans for this one world government, there is still one obstacle in the way. What—or **WHO**—is this obstacle?

Each of these topics is discussed in detail in this book and then compared to the Bible to see how prophecy is being fulfilled.

For your gift of $5.95 plus $1.25 postage and handling.
116 pages • ISBN: 1-891117-00-9

Pathway to Peace

This book has been prepared to help souls find the way to salvation and to find rest and true peace through applying God's never-failing words to our hearts. A great witnessing tool!

For your gift of $2.50 plus $1.25 postage and handling.
50 books for $50.00 plus $6.00 postage and handling.
72 pages • ISBN: 1-891117-14-9

SECURE IN CHRIST

In this most fascinating and Scripturally-oriented book you will find approximately 1000 Bible verses to meditate upon. It will enlighten you as you search the Scriptures and will encourage a closer walk with the Lord.

This book will also strengthen your spiritual outlook on life as you see how the Lord wants you to cast all your care upon Him and walk hand in hand in fellowship with Him as He leads you into the deep truth of His Word.

"Now unto Him that is able to keep you from falling, and to present you faultless before the presence of His glory with exceeding joy" (Jude 1:24).

For your gift of $6.95 plus $1.25 postage and handling.

136 pages • ISBN: 1-891117-10-6

This important book looks at the issue of speaking in tongues from a Biblical perspective. The chapters are: 1. Do All Speak in Tongues?; 2. Baptism in the Holy Ghost; 3. Sinful Lives and Tongues; 4. Signs and Wonders; 5. Prosperity and Riches; 6. The Power of Words; 7. Can We Create Our Own Reality?; 8. What Is Visualization?; 9. A Look at Inner Healing; 10. Are You a God?; 22. Misfits Removed; 12. Renegades Excluded!; 13. Thy Kingdom Come!; and 14. Will the Church Be Raptured?

For your gift of only $8.95 plus $1.25 postage and handling.

ISBN: 1-891117-18-1

STARTLING FACTS ABOUT AA UNCOVERED

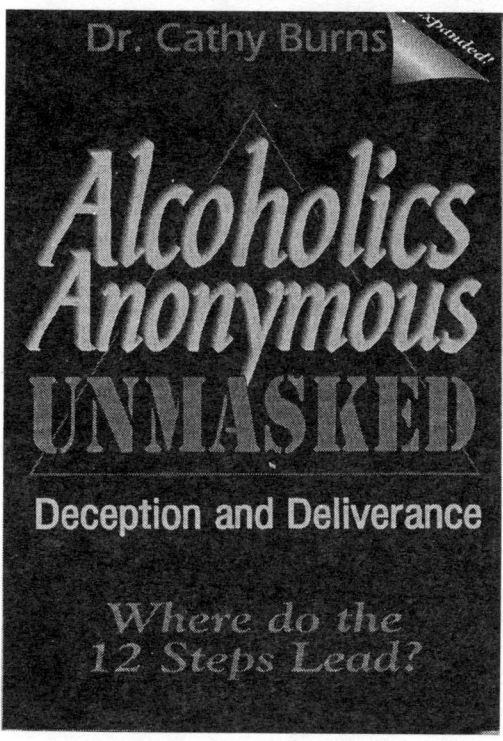

- Who is the Higher Power of AA?
- Were AA's founders Christians or occultists?
- How is the New Age involved?
- Is there a "Rockefeller connection"?
- Who are AA's "godparents"?
- How successful is AA's treatment program?
- Is alcoholism a sin or a disease?

Don't you think it's time to learn about Bill Wilson's adulterous affairs, LSD experimentation, as well as his and Dr. Bob Smith's interest in seances and spiritualism?

320 pages • $11.95 • ISBN 1-56043-449-X

A SCRIPTURAL VIEW OF HELL

Dr. Cathy Burns

Does the Bible teach soul sleep?
Is Hell eternal?
Is Hell the grave?
Are the wicked annihilated?
Is there fire in Hell?
Is Hell a place of torment?
All of these questions are answered Scripturally in this small book.

For your gift of $4.95 plus $1.05 postage and handling.

40 pages • ISBN: 1-891117-11-4

Billy Graham and His Friends

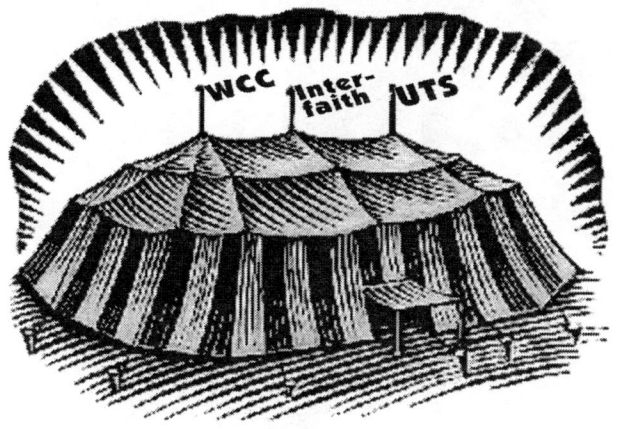

This fasincating book covers many aspects of Billy Graham's life that cannot be found elsewhere. You will discover some little known facts about one of the most well-known men of the 20th century—as well as several of his influential friends. This adventure will take us inside Graham's tent meetings and crusades, his visits to other countries, and his friendship with many Presidents and national leaders.

While Graham has been a beacon of hope in spiritually turbulent times and the source of comfort and solace to many in times of tragedy, we find that others have questioned his connection with the National and World Council of Churches, as well as the ecumenical movement. Using many of his own quotes, you will be able to find out about the other side of Billy Graham and find out about some things that have taken place "behind the scenes." This is your opportunity to take a look at this unusual man.

This book also gives brief reports (appx. 1 to 3 pages each) on dozens of people and subjects such as: Martin Luther King, Jr., Dietrich Bonhoeffer, Bishop Fulton Sheen, Amy Grant, Nelson Mandela, Al Gore, Henry Luce, Laurence Rockefeller, The Alpha Course, Prince of Egypt, Harry Potter, Vatican II, Jesse Jackson, Mikhail Gorbachev, Pope Paul VI, Pope John Paul II, Harry Ward, E. V. Hill, Bishop James Pike, Elvis Presley, Billy Kim, Chuck Colson, C. S. Lewis, Madeleine L'Engle, Archbishop George Carey, Mother Teresa, John R. W. Stott, Tony Campolo, John Marks Templeton, WCC/FCC/NCC, Robert Schuller, John Foster Dulles, Andrew Young, Desmond Tutu, Norman Vincent Peale, Virginia Ramey Mollenkott, Teilhard de Chardin, Armand Hammer, National Endowment for the Arts, United Bible Societies, United Nations Meditation Room, Union Theological Seminary, etc., etc.

For your gift of $21.95 plus $2.20 postage and handling.
800 pages (with Index) Over 4400 footnotes • ISBN:1-891117-17-3

Intriguing Mysteries Exposed!

♦ Who founded the Eastern Star and **WHY**?

♦ Is it a secret society shrouded in obscurity?

♦ Is it compatible with Christianity?

♦ What is the meaning of the Cabalistic Motto?

♦ **WHO** is represented by the Star in the East?

♦ Is there a **GODDESS** connection?

Over 100 pictures are included as well as 1453 footnotes, many taken directly from Eastern Star and Masonic sources.

This book takes you inside the Lodge room and on a journey through the five degrees. Secret passwords are revealed as well as the hidden meaning of symbols, colors, flowers, and gems, and the significance of the lambskin apron.

A special section is included on the *Rainbow Girls*.

For your gift of only $15.95 plus $1.55 shipping and handling.

512 pages (with Index) • ISBN 0-00502-181-2

SHOCKING TRUTH REVEALED

√   Does Masonry promote astrology and reincarnation?

√   Are Masonry and Christianity compatible?

√   What do the Masonic symbols represent?

√   Who is the **REAL** god of Masonry?

Discover hidden meanings, sexual overtones, the god they conceal, and much more. Fully documented with 276 footnotes.

64 pages • $4.95 (plus $1.25 postage) • ISBN 0-00-540512-2

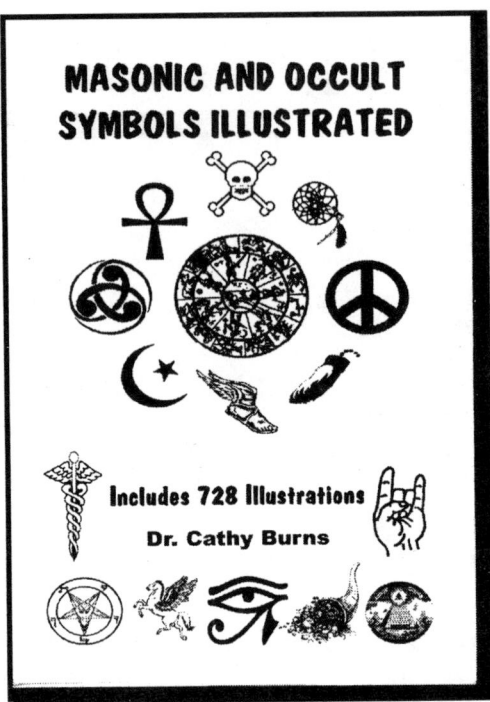

CAPTIVATING AND UNIQUE!!!

Discover the most fasincating and in-depth meanings behind the symbols used by the Masons, occultists, witches, New Agers, Satanists, and others.

Dr. Burns uncovers the hidden meanings behind the symbols that we see around us every day. In this well-document book you will see hundreds of illustrations along with their explanations. You will find many organizational logos, hand signals, tarot cards, zodiac signs, talismans, amulets, and humanist symbols, as well as the meaning of the peace symbol, hexagram, pentagram, yin/yang, circle, all-seeing eye, caduceus, oroboros, ankh, triskele, and the triangle. Also revealed in this book are numerous Masonic and Eastern Star symbols, such as the clasped hands, point within a circle, broken column, gavel, obelisk, pomegranate, and the cornucopia.

Only $21.95 • 552 pages (with Index) • ISBN 1-891117-12-2